Napoleon
The Legend and the Reality

Duncan MacIntyre

Blackie

GENERAL EDITOR:
Duncan MacIntyre
Senior Lecturer in History
Jordanhill College of Education
Glasgow

For MARTHA and GEORGE

Educational Edition   ISBN 0 216 90179 0
General Edition   ISBN 0 216 90193 6

PUBLISHED BY:
Blackie & Son Limited
Bishopbriggs, Glasgow G64 2NZ
450/452 Edgware Road, London W2 1EG

PRINTED IN GREAT BRITAIN BY:
Robert MacLehose & Co. Ltd, Glasgow

General Editor's Preface

Contrasts in History is designed for use by students preparing for G.C.E. O Level and S.C.E. O Grade examinations. The volumes in the series could also be used for work of a more advanced nature.

Although the need to provide a narrative framework is not overlooked, the real intention is that each volume, by identifying and analysing problems, should introduce readers to the complexities of historical personalities and situations.

It is hoped that a series which illustrates the many-sided nature of events and periods, examines contrasts within and between societies, demonstrates the interplay of change and continuity, and seeks to create an awareness of differing interpretations, will help to build up a sense of the past and encourage the development of thinking skills.

DUNCAN MACINTYRE

Acknowledgments

The author and publisher wish to thank the following for permission to reproduce the photographs listed below.

Photographie Giraudon, Paris: *page 5*
Trustees of the British Museum: *page 25 (top)*
Victoria & Albert Museum: *page 25 (foot)*
Museum of Fine Arts, Boston: *page 57*

Plates
The Mansell Collection: *pages (i) & (ii)*
Bulloz, Paris: *page (iii)*
Bibliothéque Nationale: *page (iv)*

Contents

The Bonapartes

CHARLES-MARIE BONAPARTE = MARIE-LAETITIA RAMOLINO
died 1785 / died 1836

JOSEPH, King of Naples 1806–1808; King of Spain 1808–1813 died 1844

NAPOLEON I born 1769 First Consul 1799 Emperor 1804 died 1821
(1) = JOSEPHINE divorced 1809 died 1814 (= (previously) ALEXANDRE DE BEAUHARNAIS)
(2) = MARIE LOUISE, daughter of Francis II of Austria died 1847

NAPOLEON (II) King of Rome 1811–1814 Duke of Reichstadt died 1832

EUGÈNE Viceroy of Italy died 1824

HORTENSE died 1837 = LOUIS King of Holland 1806–1810 died 1846

LUCIEN died 1840

CAROLINE died 1839 = JOACHIM MURAT, Grand Duke of Berg 1806 King of Naples 1808 executed 1815

JEROME King of Westphalia 1807–1813 died 1860

Prince Napoleon died 1891 = CLOTILDE, daughter of Victor Emmanuel II of Piedmont

(LOUIS) **NAPOLEON III** born 1808 President 1848–1852 Emperor 1852–1870 died 1873 = EUGÉNIE de MONTIJO died 1920

LOUIS NAPOLEON, Prince Imperial killed in action 1879

1

The Legend

St Helena is a volcanic rock rising out of the South Atlantic Ocean, 1900 kilometres from the west coast of Africa. It is far distant from the plains of northern Italy, Germany and Russia; from the mountains of Spain and the streets of Paris. Seventeen kilometres long by ten and a half wide, it has an area of one hundred and twenty-two square kilometres. As such it is about one third of the size of the Isle of Wight. On 17 October 1815, H.M.S. *Northumberland* dropped anchor at St Helena and Napoleon Bonaparte went into exile. His glories were behind him. His word, which had once carried from France to Spain and Italy in the south, to Belgium and Holland in the north, to Germany and Poland in the east, was no longer law. But the world was not rid of him, for

the last, but not the least of Napoleon's victories was won at St Helena.[1]

This victory was not one of arms and men. Napoleon's "army" on the island consisted of a few servants, the families of Comte Bertrand and Charles Montholon, Comte Las Cases and his son, General Gourgaud and Dr Barry O'Meara. As death and departures reduced the ranks, reinforcements arrived in the shape of two servants, two priests and another physician. Surrounding them was a British military garrison of 3000 men. The victory had to be one of ideas, the ideas which laid the foundation for the Napoleonic Legend.

In October 1820, with his health failing in the last few months of his life, Napoleon remarked to Montholon: "There is no more oil in the lamp." But the flame was not extinguished. Through Dr O'Meara's *A Voice from St Helena*, Las Cases' *The Memorial of St Helena*, and Montholon's *History of the Captivity of Napoleon*, a splendid memory was created, polished and preserved. Of course, the problem with memories, however splendid, is that "history experienced and history remembered are two different things".

As one would expect, there was the image of Napoleon as the supreme military genius. Misfortune and defeat in battle were rare.

When they did occur it was because of betrayal or the failings of subordinates rather than of misjudgments on the part of Napoleon or superior strategy and tactics on the part of the enemy.

Then there was the claim that the Napoleonic wars were not of the Emperor's choosing. From St Helena came the message that Napoleon was an apostle of peace.

All my victories and all my conquests were won in self-defence . . . Europe never ceased from warring against France, against French principles, and against me. So we had to strike down in order not to be struck down.[2]

If Europe was torn by war during the fifteen years of his rule, the responsibility did not lie with him.

For all that I held the rudder, and with so strong a hand, the waves were a good deal stronger. I never was, in truth, my own master. I was always governed by circumstances.[2]

The essence of this argument is that the foreign and military policy of Napoleon was the inevitable product of circumstances created by the Revolutionary governments which had preceded him. In October 1795, the Convention annexed Belgium and the Rhineland and so pushed France forward to the so-called "natural frontiers" of the Rhine and the Alps. In doing this, the Convention prepared a course for Napoleon from which he could not deviate; a course which in honour he could not abandon. The natural frontiers had been won. They now had to be defended. To do this, Napoleon had to fight, since the other powers—Britain in particular—would never consent that these frontiers should remain with France. It was not his wish to wage war. But he had no say in the matter.

And what of France? "I swear that I do nothing except for France," said Napoleon before his fall. And on his lonely rock, reliving the glories of his past, he was still in no doubt.

I governed for the entire community, for the whole great French family.[3]

In his will he urged that his son should adopt the motto which had ever been in the forefront of his father's mind:

Everything for the French people.[4]

But what of the Revolution? "*I am the Revolution*," Napoleon insisted at the height of his power and, on St Helena, Montholon recorded the exile's words:

I have saved the Revolution, which was on the point of death; I have washed off its crimes, I have held it up to the eyes of Europe, resplendent with glory.[3]

The image is of a man who first of all rescued from possible extinction,

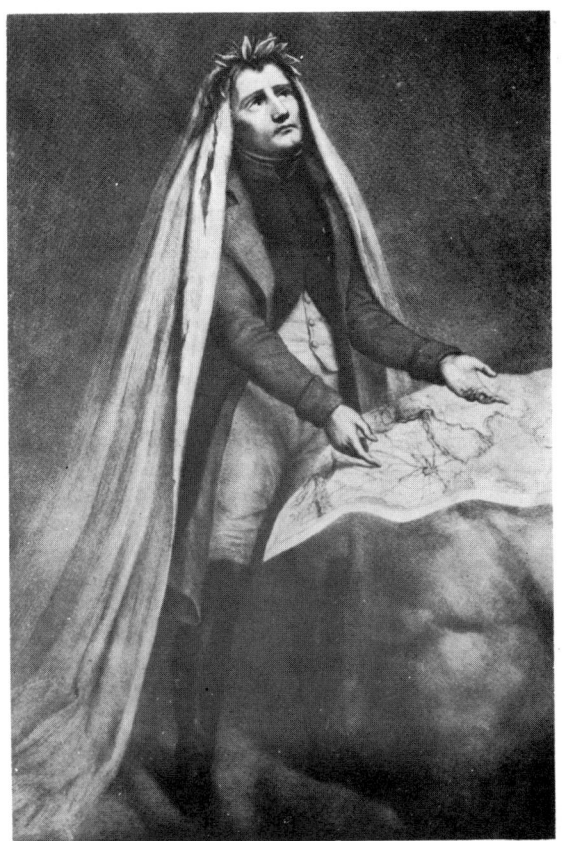

"Moreover I will endeavour that ye may be able after my decease to have these things always in remembrance." (Peter II, I, v. 15.) This painting, with its biblical caption, is one of the more exotic expressions of the Legend.

then consolidated, the great ideals of the Revolution. The suggestion is that there was a sort of kinship between the Revolutionary and Napoleonic periods, so that the real "spirit" of each was essentially the same.

To round the story off, Napoleon was presented as a man whose career was a struggle on behalf of the peoples of Europe against the dynasts of Europe. He was cast in the part of liberator. The cause of national feeling had been deliberately stimulated. In other words, Napoleonic conquest was the Revolution on the march, the means by which new and progressive doctrines and ideals were consciously exported to other, less favoured lands.

Our enemies, he dictated on St Helena, *are the enemies of mankind. They want to put chains around the people, whom they regard as a herd . . .*[3]

How would men respond to this splendid memory? Here was a question which concerned Napoleon. He convinced himself that all would be well.

Is there any point on which I could be attacked and on which a historian could not take up my defence? he asked Las Cases.

Q: My despotism?

A: He can prove that dictatorship was absolutely necessary.

Q: Will it be said that I restricted freedom?

A: He will be able to prove that licence, anarchy and general disorder were still on our doorstep.

Q: Shall I be accused of having loved war too much?

A: He will show that I was always on the defensive.

Q: (Will it be said) that I wanted to set up a universal monarchy?

A: He will explain that it was . . . the result of circumstances and that I was led to it step by step by our . . . enemies.[3]

How did men respond? It is probably true that ". . . few historians have not been mesmerized into accepting at least some of these lines". In the nineteenth century, the thoughts of many French writers were coloured by the nature of the times in which they lived, and the political viewpoint of a particular historian often decided whether he would idolize or condemn the Napoleonic era. Of course, there were others who attempted a purely critical analysis, who set the Legend against the reality, as they saw it, in order to measure the extent of correspondence or divergence.

With Napoleon gone there was something dull about the present and something glorious about the past. For "no nation in modern times had achieved such military glory as had France during the brief span from 1796 to 1812". The pride and indignation of one French historian took the following form:

The glory of Napoleon is a national possession. Whoever touches it defaces the nation itself.[2]

The exile had guessed correctly when he said ". . . whenever they want to strike a lofty attitude, they will praise me".

And so his memory lived on, being carefully nurtured. In 1831, Alexandre Dumas' play *Napoleon Bonaparte* was performed in Paris. Among other things, the play dealt with the quarrel between Napoleon and the Governor of St Helena, Sir Hudson Lowe. The alleged cruelty of the Governor aroused such bitter emotions in the audience that the actor playing the part had to receive police protection.

This 1832 medallion reflects the influence of the Legend. It is the young, energetic, conquering Bonaparte who is being commemorated.

In 1854, Napoleon III, the nephew of the great man, set up a Commission

> to collect, classify, and publish the correspondence of our august predecessor, Napoleon I . . .[5]

The 15 volumes which were published contained 13,094 of Bonaparte's letters and dispatches. However, some of the documents did not tie in with the Legend as created on St Helena, and so, in 1864, the Commission was re-formed. The new editors omitted many letters from its publications. No mention was made of instructions to the Minister of Police ordering arrests or imprisonments; letters dealing with the censorship of the press were ignored, as were orders to generals for the burning of villages and the execution of rebels.

And in times of defeat or humiliation Frenchmen remembered the Emperor. The military disaster of the Franco-Prussian War (1870–71) was such an occasion.

> A defeated or humbled France can no more forget Lodi, the Pyramids, Austerlitz . . . than the Israelites by the waters of Babylon could forget Jerusalem.[3]

The Legend has not gone unchallenged. Certain doubts have been expressed about Napoleon's military skill. The claim that he fought defensively whilst all along wanting peace has been questioned by historians who consider that Napoleon's wars were his own wars, made inevitable not by the annexations of 1795 but by his own measureless greed and lust for glory. Against the image of Napoleon as the ruler thinking only of the welfare of France we have Taine's

5

view that although the Emperor loved France, this love was like that of a horseman for his animal. All the grooming and the care was not really for the benefit of the horse, but to prepare it as a useful creature for the service of the rider. To those who support the Legend of Napoleon as the protector and consolidator of the Revolution many others answer that he was the destroyer, the betrayer and the debaser of the Revolution. Alphonse Aulard saw him as the man who arrested the Revolution and pushed France back towards the *ancien régime*. Against the view that Napoleon consciously stimulated national feeling in the conquered lands and brought freedom to the peoples of Europe there is the suggestion that "the Napoleonic Empire was the negation of nationality".

This contrast between the Legend as publicized by Las Cases, O'Meara and Montholon—then developed in later years—and the reality of Napoleon's life and work, as seen by others, presents one of the most intriguing problems of modern history. The difficulty lies in the fact that one man's version of reality may differ from that of another. Yet it is a difficulty which must be tackled. "The mists of St Helena" should not be allowed to "obscure the figure of Napoleon".

Bonaparte had, of course, been a fascinating figure before his exile. The dramatic contrasts associated with his name are not exhausted by those between ". . . a real renown and . . . an imaginary one". From humble enough origins in Corsica he scaled incredible heights, so that between 1799 and 1815

it was he who dominated history.[6]

From 1796, when as a general he began his successful campaigns in Italy, to 1810

. . . everything seemed to yield before him.[6]

And then there was the fall, so that success and "the element of disaster" went together.

No name stands so conspicuously for victory, glory and catastrophe.[7]

The administrator and the general are usually separate individuals, each working in his own area. With Napoleon those contrasting functions were merged in the one person, so that

as a man of action he remains unique . . . No man after him has combined outstanding military genius as a leader in the field with a political career on a world scale.[4]

Even when campaigning all over Europe and in the thick of strategic and tactical business he still concerned himself with the day to day problems of administering France and his Empire. Over 41,000 of his letters and instructions have been published. Many have not been made public; many others have been lost or destroyed. It is estimated that during the 15 years of his rule he wrote between 60,000 and 70,000, making an average of about twelve a day.

From Baron Meneval, his secretary from 1802 to 1813, we get an impression of Bonaparte at work:

Sometimes Napoleon would work alone from 2 a.m.–5 a.m. and begin to dictate at 7; sometimes, when there was a press of business, the secretary would be summoned at 4 a.m. or 5 a.m. and find Napoleon waiting for him—for an hour or two he would dictate with amazing fluence and clearness, and so rapidly that it was necessary to invent a kind of short-hand . . . when this early spell of dictation was over, Napoleon would . . . go to bed again. After an hour's sleep he would be ready for the real work of the day.[5]

Bourrienne, his secretary from 1797 to 1802, fills in the other details:

From breakfast at 10 a.m. to dinner at 5 p.m. every hour was taken up with reading petitions, correcting letters, giving interviews, or attending meetings.[5]

Complex and many sided, there was nothing flat or dull about Napoleon's personality. There was, on the one hand, charm, sensitivity and generosity. In August 1794 the Robespierrists fell from power in France, and Bonaparte, who had been acquainted with them, was imprisoned for a short time. A certain Saliceti, who had played some part in his imprisonment, afterwards found that he himself was a fugitive and took refuge with Madame Permon. Napoleon wrote the following letter on 18 June 1795:

I know Saliceti has been hidden in your house now for more than three weeks.

You see, Saliceti, I could have returned evil for the evil you did me, and could have had my revenge; whereas the harm you did me was entirely unprovoked. Which of us is playing the hero now—you, or I? Yes, I might have had my revenge, but I chose not to. Go, then, and seek undisturbed for a refuge in which you can recover a more patriotic state of mind. I shall not say a word about you, now or ever. Repent, and (above all) appreciate my motives as they deserve, for they are noble and generous.[5]

A letter to Josephine, dated 5 April 1796, begins:

It is an hour after midnight. They bring me a letter. It is a sad one, and my soul is touched: for Chauvet is dead. He was our Q.M.G.[5]

The widows of dead comrades were not forgotten. On the night of 1 August 1798, Admiral Brueys was killed in the action between the British and French fleets at Aboukir Bay. Napoleon's letter to Madame Brueys is gentle and encouraging.

Your sorrow touches me to the quick. It is a dreadful moment when we are parted from one we love. It shuts us off from the world. The body is convulsed with pain, and the faculties of the mind so overwhelmed that all its contacts with reality are cut off by a distorting dream. Things are such that, if there were no reason for living, it were better to die. But when second thoughts supervene, and you press your children to your heart, your nature is revived by tears and tenderness, and you live for the sake of your offspring. Yes, Madame, you will weep with them, you will nurture their infancy, you will educate their youth; you will speak to them of their father and of your grief, of their loss and of the Republic's. And when you have linked your soul to the world again through the mutual affection of mother and child, I want you to count as of some value my friendship, and the lively interest that I shall always take in the wife of my friend. Be assured that there are men—a minority—who can turn grief into hope, because they feel so intimately the troubles of the heart.[5]

Generosity was even extended to the enemy. In a dispatch of 12 November 1811, the Emperor wrote:

Whilst I was crossing the river at Givet, a detachment of English prisoners was at work repairing a pontoon bridge. I noticed particularly the keenness and activity of eight or ten of these men, who jumped into a small boat to help get the bridge into position. Order a list to be made of the ten men who distinguished themselves most in this affair.[5]

Each man was given new clothes, money, and a safe conduct home.

This aspect of Napoleon's personality could still be observed when he became a captive in 1815. "Damn the fellow," said Admiral Lord Keith. "If he had obtained an interview with His Royal Highness in half an hour they would have been the best friends in England."

On the other hand, he was also capable of harshness and could lack sympathy.

RAMBOUILLET, *7 September 1807*

You must be sure to inform Marshal Soult, by special messenger, of the incident of Königsberg, where two actors appearing on the stage as French officers, were hissed by the audience. You will tell Marshal Soult that I have demanded satisfaction from the King of Prussia for this insult, and that I have required that the two chief culprits shall be shot. Marshal Soult is to inform the officer opposite him of the base and despicable character of the outrage of which I have had to complain, and of the explicit terms in which I have demanded satisfaction.[5]

In 1809, Louise, the ex-Queen of Spain, who had made her home in France, became ill, and the clergy of Provence offered prayers for her recovery. Napoleon's response was immediate.

Inform me why the Archbishop of Aix has ordered nine days' intercession for the illness of Queen Louise, and why the general public should be told to pray for anyone without the permission of the Government.[5]

Before and after coming to power he demonstrated that there was a ruthless side to his personality.

To General Berthier

HEADQUARTERS, CAIRO, *23 October 1798*

Instruct the officer in command of the place to decapitate all prisoners taken with arms in their hands. They are to be taken to-night to the bank of the Nile between Boulâq and Old Cairo; and their headless bodies are to be thrown into the river.[5]

To General Savary, Duke of Rovigo, Minister of Police

COMPIÈGNE, *12 September 1811*

Have the wife of the pilot Gallet, who is in the English service, arrested, and write to him saying that, unless he either returns to France, or goes to live in a neutral country under conditions guaranteeing that he is not in English pay, she and her children will be put in prison, in solitary confinement, and fed on bread and water. Apply the same measure to the wives and families of all pilots in the English service. Present me with a decree to this effect, and have an inquiry made as to the pilots who are on board enemy ships.[5]

When studying a complex character like Bonaparte, and setting legend against reality so that the extent to which the two coincide or diverge may be tested, it would be wrong to imagine that final answers will ever be found. Pieter Geyl's *Napoleon: For and Against* examines the interpretations of 47 writers. In this mass of material, much of it conflicting, some readers may have expected to find the whole truth about the man. For them the concluding sentence, after 400 pages, must have been a disappointment. It is simply, "The argument goes on". And it still goes on. What is read here will not end it. "Truth, though for God it may be one, assumes many shapes to men."

---

[1] *New Cambridge Modern History* (NCMH) Volume IX; [2] *Napoleon: For and Against* by P. Geyl (CAPE); [3] *The Age of Napoleon* by Christopher Herold (PENGUIN); [4] *Napoleon* by F. Markham (WEIDENFELD & NICOLSON); [5] *Napoleon Bonaparte* letters translated by J. M. Thompson (DENT); [6] *Napoleon* Volume 1 by G. Lefebvre (ROUTLEDGE & KEGAN PAUL); [7] *Napoleon and Europe* by L. C. F. Turner (WARNE).

2

A Great Master of War

The French historian, Louis Madelin, considered that Napoleon was ". . . a great master of war", who ". . . towered above Caesar himself and . . . far surpassed all who had gone before". This view has always been widely accepted. During the early months of the First World War, as the opposing sides settled into trenches on the Western Front and deadlock became more and more difficult to break, General de Castelnau is reported to have said,

A, Napoleon, Napoleon. If he were here now he'd have thought of the "something else".[1]

Castelnau was voicing the popular opinion that Napoleon, with his imagination and genius, would have found a solution to the problem of trench warfare. He would have thought of the "something else" which had eluded the British, French and German commanders in 1914. The Legend had developed deep roots. This is not surprising when it is remembered that from 1796 to 1815 Napoleon campaigned throughout Europe, and that for much of that time he had a remarkable record of success. There is some truth in the claim that ". . . for Frenchmen who survived them, those were unforgettable days. Even under Louis XIV, France had not known such glory and grandeur, or such power."

However, the popular view of Napoleon must not be accepted at its face value. Important questions have to be asked. Were the successes solely due to Napoleon's genius as a military commander, as the Legend would have us believe? Was he in fact ". . . a great master of war"? Did he always think of the "something else"?

Napoleon has been praised for the tactics which he used in battle and for the enthusiasm which he was able to encourage in his soldiers. Yet the enthusiasm was there before he took command and the tactics came from the minds of other men.

The armies raised by French governments between 1792 and 1795 to defend the Revolution against its enemies were very different from those raised by previous French rulers or by the monarchs of Austria, Prussia and· Russia. Karl von Clausewitz, the German military writer, noted that before the French Revolution, wars in the eighteenth century had been "wars of kings, not of peoples". No king could call on the devotion and enthusiasm of all his subjects, for his wars were ". . . entirely separated from the interests of the people". For the French, 1789 changed all this. Men were no longer subjects, but citizens, with rights and liberties to defend against foreign enemies who sought to destroy the precious gains of the Revolution. In Clausewitz's words,

> *war had . . . suddenly become an affair of the people, and that of a people numbering thirty millions, every one of whom regarded himself as a citizen. . . .*[2]

It was now possible for French governments to call on every individual, man, woman and child, to play his part in the war effort. Nothing demonstrates this more than the decree issued by the Convention on 23 August 1793. The repetition of the words "all" and "everyone" is striking. No one is excluded. Age and sex is not a disqualification.

> *. . . Let us state a great truth: liberty has become the creditor of all citizens. Some owe it their labour, others their wealth, some their counsel, others the strength of their arms; all owe it the blood which flows in their veins. Thus all the French, men and women alike, people of all ages, are summoned by the Patrie to defend liberty. All physical and moral faculties, all political and industrial means, belong to it by right; all metals, all elements, pay it their tribute. Let everyone take up his post; let everyone behave as he should in this national and military uprising . . . and all will soon be proud that they had worked together to save the Patrie. . . .*
>
> *Thus all are requisitioned, but all will not march off to war. Some will make weapons, others will use them; some will prepare food supplies for combatants, others will sacrifice their clothing and what they most need themselves. Men, women, children, in requisitioning you the Patrie summons you all in the name of liberty; . . . and it designates to each of you according to his means the services he must give to the armies of the Republic.*
>
> *Young men will fight, young men are called to conquer. Married men will forge arms, transport military baggage and guns and will prepare food supplies. Women, who at long last are to take their rightful place in the revolution and follow their true destiny, will forget their futile tasks: their delicate hands will work at making clothes for soldiers; they will make tents. . . . Children will make lint of old cloth. It is for them that we are fighting. . . . And old men, performing their missions again, as of*

yore, will be guided to the public squares of the cities where they will kindle the courage of young warriors and preach the doctrines of hate for kings and the unity of the Republic.

Napoleon inherited this spirit of devotion and total commitment. He did not create it. In fairness, however, it must be said that he realized how valuable it was and did his best to keep the flame burning. Friend and enemy alike paid tribute to his ability in this respect. The Saxon officer, Captain von Odeleben, said,

At times Napoleon's words affected the troops like witchcraft.[3]

and his most celebrated opponent, the Duke of Wellington, confessed,

There was nothing like him. His presence on the battlefield was worth 40,000 men.[3]

An early history of Napoleon, published in 1825, described his relationship with his soldiers:

. . . he would find out if any officers' places had fallen vacant, and ask in a loud voice the names of the men most worthy to fill them. He called up the men who were pointed out to him and he proceeded to interrogate them: How many years of service did they have? What campaigns had they been through? What wounds had they suffered? Had they performed any brilliant deeds? He then promoted them officers and had them commissioned there and then in his presence . . . all these little details were calculated to entrance the soldiers.[4]

The skill with which Napoleon fired the imagination and unleashed the energies of his troops is seen in his Order of the Day issued to the Army of Italy from his headquarters at Milan on 20 May 1796. He praises them for victories already won, tells them of the pride which their countrymen feel in their exploits, promises that future hardships will lead to even greater glory and that their fame will never die. They are made to feel important, invincible, and immortal.

SOLDIERS,

You have rushed like a torrent from the heights of the Apennines: you have overthrown, dispersed and scattered everything that opposed your advance . . .

Such success has brought joy to the heart of our country. There, your fathers, your mothers, your wives, your sisters, your sweethearts are rejoicing in your successes and proudly proclaim that they belong to you. Yes, Soldiers, you have done much; but there is still much to do. Well, then, let us go. There are still forced marches to be made, enemies to be defeated, laurels to be won, insults to avenge. . . . Then you will return to your homes, and your fellow citizens will point you out and say: "He was of the Army of Italy."

Though this is a rousing appeal it should be remembered that Napoleon was building upon an enthusiasm which already existed. The Legend is silent on this point.

The greatness of military commanders is sometimes measured by the battle tactics which they have devised. Yet a leading historian of armed forces and the art of war has argued that

> *Napoleon was not a great military reformer . . . (his) tactical views . . . owed more to the reformers of Louis XVI's reign and to the practice of the early revolutionary armies than to Napoleon himself.*[2]

Two military theorists in particular, writing before the French Revolution, defined the tactics which were later used by Napoleon. It had been the custom in eighteenth-century warfare, irrespective of the nature of the terrain, for the infantry of opposing armies to take up "line formation" facing each other:

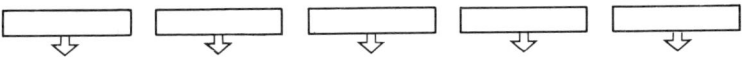

The Comte de Guibert, in his *General Essay on Tactics* published in 1772, argued that this method was wasteful of time, and once put into operation was difficult to alter if the need arose.

> *In the tactics of thirty years ago and of some armies today, the movements for forming a line of battle were so slow and complicated that they took hours. The line had to be formed at a safe distance from the enemy, and once the formation had been taken up it was dangerous to attempt to change it.*[2]

It was his view that under certain circumstances an infantry "column" could be much more effective and mobile than the line. The column had three distinct advantages. It could be formed more speedily than a line; once formed it could be used to smash its way through an opposing line of infantry, and the column, having brought troops close to the enemy, could be transformed into a line without waste of time.

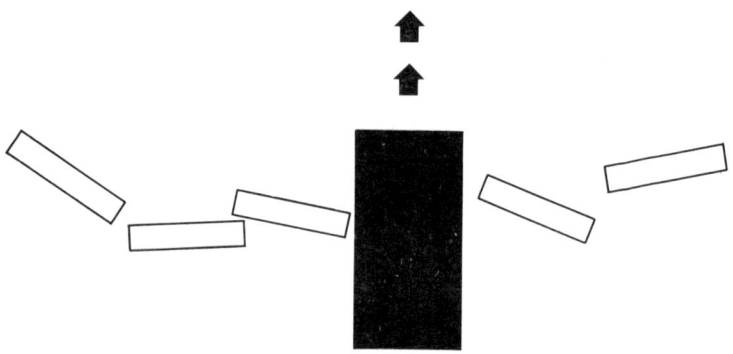

It had also been the practice for armies to march along pre-arranged routes followed by long supply trains. Ahead, on the line of the march, supply units would be laying down dumps of provisions for the army in what were known as "prepared magazines". This meant that an army's lines of communication and direction were to a large extent determined by the exact location of supplies. Troops could neither afford to march so fast that they would move too far ahead of slow supply trains, nor take routes which had no prepared magazines. This forced armies into routines which reduced opportunities to do the unexpected. The elements of surprise and mobility were being ignored. It was such elements which Guibert wished to restore to military practice. Armies could be released from the strait-jacket if they forgot about supply trains and magazines and lived off the land, requisitioning their needs from the areas through which they marched.

What I want to avoid, wrote Guibert, *is that my supplies should command me. . . . The enemy must see me marching when he supposes me fettered by the calculation of my supplies . . .*[2]

The Chevalier du Teil, in a book on the use of artillery published in 1778, urged that batteries should be concentrated rather than dispersed, and that they should be used for specific purposes.

. . . we ought never to engage in artillery duels, except when it is indispensable for the protection of our troops, but that on the contrary our principal purpose must be, as has been said, to fire on the enemy's troops, when we can destroy them or the obstacles which cover them.[2]

While at the Military Academy at Brienne between April 1779 and the summer of 1784, and at the Military Academy in Paris between October 1784 and September 1785, Napoleon absorbed the ideas of the military thinkers and when in 1796 he was given command of the army destined for Italy he was prepared to put them into practice.

The Napoleonic Legend becomes slightly less impressive when it is realized that in the enthusiastic armies provided by the Revolution and in the writings of Guibert and du Teil, Bonaparte found both the instrument and the tactics for his success in battle. Yet the most spirited soldiers and the most effective tactics can be misused. Inspiration may be necessary if things are to be made to work. When Napoleon remarked that "everything is in the execution", he was probably underestimating the advantages placed within his grasp, but he was nevertheless making a valid point. In the hands of an incompetent general, advantages may mean nothing. In Napoleon's hands they could mean everything, and in many cases the use he made of them was outstanding.

In favourable circumstances he moved his armies at greater speed and with more emphasis on manoeuvrability than any other general of the period. He was seldom riveted to routine. His ability to improvise was considerable. He saw each battle as a unique occasion with its own special features and conditions, for example the extent of the front, the nature of the terrain, the number of men available. There is no doubt that in many instances he was a master of the art of creating or conjuring up a decisive superiority at a crucial moment in time. The Battle of Castiglione, 6 August 1796, demonstrates those gifts at work in the early stages of his career.

Where roads were good and the surrounding countryside could provide supplies for his soldiers, Napoleon followed the advice of Guibert. He split his forces into separate units and sent them off along different routes in search of the enemy. When and where a unit encountered opponents it would act on its instructions to pin them down in that area, so that a fixed point was provided on which the rest of the French army could concentrate. Stated simply, Napoleon's plan was "to march divided and fight united".

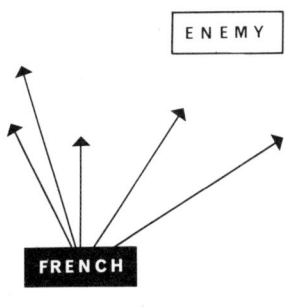

March Divided

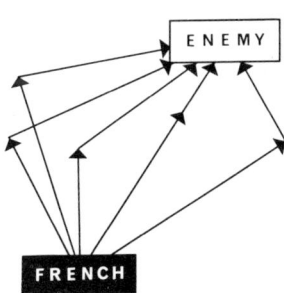

Fight United

Battle of Castiglione

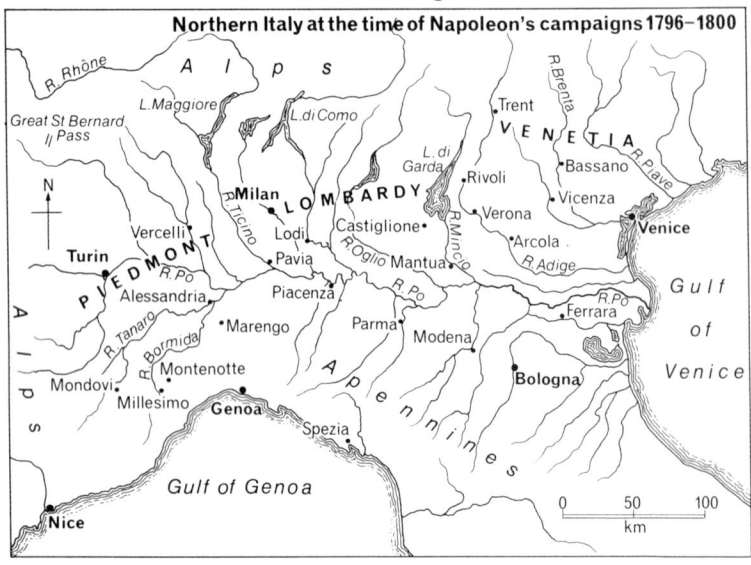

Northern Italy at the time of Napoleon's campaigns 1796–1800

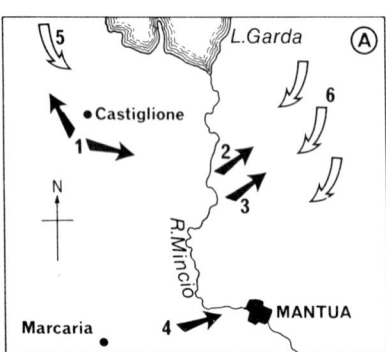

Napoleon's forces are spread out, and threatened by attack from west and east.

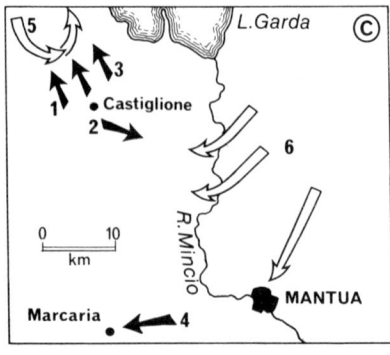

Now having more strength in the region of Castiglione, Napoleon threw most of his forces against Quasdanovitch and so destroyed the Austrian threat in the west. He was aided in carrying out this tactic by the fact that Wurmser marched slowly and delayed in getting his troops across the River Mincio. Had Wurmser acted with greater speed Napoleon may not have been able to defeat Quasdanovitch.

In August 1796, Napoleon, as Commander-in-Chief of the French forces in Italy, had 46,000 men at his disposal. He was opposed by Austrian forces totalling 55,000 men, made up of

 (i) The army led by General Wurmser
 (ii) The army led by General Quasdanovitch
 (iii) The Austrian garrison in Mantua

The French were in a difficult position, for not only were they outnumbered, they were also facing attack from two different directions: from Wurmser in the east and from Quasdanovitch in the west.

French forces:
1 Napoleon
2 Masséna
3 Augereau
4 Serurier

Austrian forces:
5 Quasdanovitch
6 Wurmser

• Towns

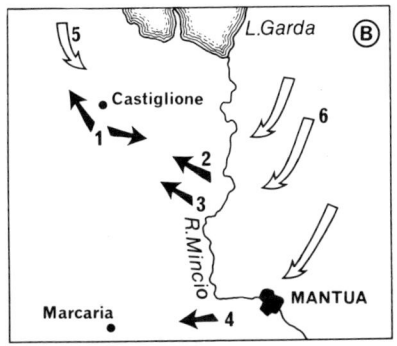

Napoleon ordered Masséna and Augereau to retreat west of the River Mincio. At the same time, he ordered Serurier to retreat along the road towards Marcaria, giving the Austrians the impression that this part of the French army would not be used in the battle.

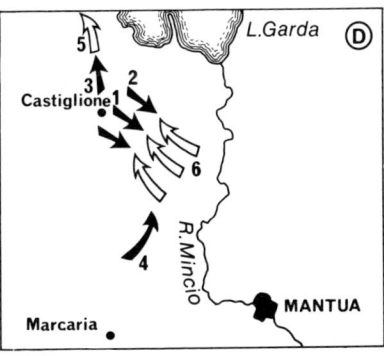

With Quasdanovitch in full retreat, pursued by a <u>small</u> French force, Napoleon turned with the major part of his army to face Wurmser. Napoleon then sent instructions to Serurier to attack Wurmser in the rear. The Austrians were then caught in the type of trap which they had tried to lay for the French.

Very often the enemy's first sight of the French was in the form of what appeared to be an isolated unit with inferior numbers, and they were tempted to "take the bait". Believing that he was dealing with an out-of-touch unit of Napoleon's army under Marshal Lannes at Jena on 13 October 1806, the commander of the Prussian army moved forward without haste, intending to gain an easy victory the next day. By that time the French forces had concentrated, were able to "fight united", and destroyed the Prussian army. Much the same thing happened at Friedland in June 1807. The Russians, faced with what seemed easy prey in a greatly outnumbered French unit, were held long enough for the concentration to take place.

Three dispatches, typical of many which he wrote, demonstrate that to his gifts of "execution" Napoleon added insights into the problems of morale and military intelligence.

To General Songis, officer commanding artillery in Egypt
16 August 1799
You should know beforehand that, in yesterday's orders, the Commander-in-Chief has put down the grant for army uniforms at double the amount actually issued. This is for public consumption, to make them think in Europe that our effectives are twice what they really are. Warn the battalions concerned not to count upon more than half their allocations.[5]

To Marshal Berthier
August 1805
I want you to have two portable boxes made, and divided into compartments, one for me and the other for yourself. They are to be so arranged that one can find out at a glance, with the help of cards, the movements of all the Austrian troops, regiment by regiment, and battalion by battalion. . . . Once a fortnight you are to send me a list of the changes that have taken place during the previous two weeks. . . .[5]

To the Minister of War
SCHÖNBRUNN, *10 October 1809*
Please write to the King of Spain, and make him understand that nothing is more contrary to military usage than to publish the strength of one's army, either in Orders and Proclamations, or in the Gazette; *that, supposing there were any reason for talking of one's forces, one ought to exaggerate them, and to make them appear redoubtable by doubling or trebling their number: whereas, in speaking of the enemy, one ought to represent his numbers as a half or a third of what they really are.[5]*

In measuring the brilliance of a general, account must be taken of his performance in unfavourable circumstances and of the quality of opposing forces and commanders. The Legend rarely describes the opposition, probably because to have done so would have diminished the glory of Napoleon. At times the opposition had serious weaknesses; had attention been drawn to them Napoleon's success might have appeared less dramatic. At times the enemy had revealed real strengths; had credit been given to them it would have been more difficult to blame Napoleon's failure on ill-luck or betrayal. In the years before 1808 the French armies had a number of important advantages. Between 1808 and 1813 the situation changed. The contrast, and Napoleon's response to it, is worth investigating for it provides a more realistic view of the ". . . master of war" than that found in the Legend.

The battles of the earlier period were fought in areas which were suited to the use of Napoleon's tactics. During the campaigns in Italy, Austria and Germany, where good road systems and fertile countryside allowed the French to march swiftly without supply trains, the enemy was usually encouraged to offer early battle and suffered early defeat. But such methods were inappropriate in the isolated, less accessible and less prosperous areas of Spain and Portugal, described by a French veteran as

> . . . a grave which swallows everything up[3]

and

> It remained to be seen how the army as a whole would fare (in 1812) on the road through Poland and Russia, where there were precious few provisions to be had, and where Napoleon was forced to rely on the old eighteenth century magazines and supply wagons.[4]

Sir Arthur Wellesley, created Viscount Wellington in 1809 (Duke 1814), used a defensive strategy in Portugal and Spain. In his own words he

> . . . wouldn't let (the French) fight a battle . . . except under dis-advantages. . . . This is the last army England has got, he said, and we must take care of it.[6]

There was a clear pattern to his movements during the Peninsular War.

1. 1808, Wellesley lands in Portugal. Defeats Junot at Vimiero.

2. Moves into Spain. Defeats Marshal Victor at Talavera, July 1809.

3. *Retreats to Portugal.* Orders the construction of strong *defensive* lines at Tôrres Vedras to protect Lisbon from attack.

4. Masséna invades Portugal. Wellington checks the French advance at Busaco, 1810, then *retreats behind the lines of Tôrres Vedras.*

The Peninsular War

(For almost a year thousands of Portuguese labourers had worked on the lines, building walls, parapets, 152 forts, gun emplacements, and digging ditches. The countryside in the region of the lines had been stripped of supplies.

For a month Masséna clung to the waterlogged, windswept fields in front of Wellington's lines while his men grew daily more ravenous and his pack . . . animals died in thousands. The British, fed from their ships, (were) snug in their entrenchments . . .[6])

     5.   Masséna returns to Spain. Wellington follows and defeats the French at Fuentes de Oñoro, 1811.

     6.   *Retreats to Portugal.*

     7.   Re-enters Spain. Defeats Marmont at Salamanca, 1812.

     8.   *Retreats to Portugal.*

     9.   Re-enters Spain. Defeats Soult at Vittoria, 1813.

    10.   Enters France 1814.

The French armies, faced by an unfamiliar strategy, becoming more and more desperately short of provisions, and harassed by Portuguese and Spanish guerrillas, suffered a string of defeats. Battles were now being fought according to a time-table which they had not written.

This was also true of the Russian campaign. When he began his great invasion in 1812 it had not been Napoleon's intention to march to Moscow. As with his earlier wars he was seeking a quick engagement and a swift victory which would bring Russia to her knees. But the enemy armies, commanded by Barclay de Tolly and Bagration retreated into the interior and tempted the French to move deeper and deeper into unfavourable conditions. Napoleon's response was not impressive.

The trouble was that (he) had left out of account the relationship between the availability of supplies and the speed of marching.[4]

He had been forced to take his army into Russia with supply convoys of thousands of wagons, yet he still wanted to march at speed. As the invading army entered Vitebsk on 28 July 1812, General de Caulaincourt described the result of such a policy:

. . . The innumerable wagons, the enormous quantity of supplies of all sorts that had been collected at such expense during the course of two years, had vanished through theft or loss, or through lack of means to bring them up. They were scattered along the roads. The rapidity of the forced marches, the shortage of harness and spare parts, the want of care, had all helped to kill the horses. This campaign at express speed from the Niemen to Wilna and from Wilna to Witebsk had, without any real result, already cost the army [the equivalent of] two lost battles and deprived it of absolutely essential provisions and supplies.[3]

The retreat was even more disastrous. Forced by Russian tactics to return along the same route taken by the invasion, the French army, constantly under attack from raiding parties, had to march wearily through a devastated countryside which could not sustain it. It is, of course, easy to look back on events and be critical of Napoleon's decisions. Yet "a great military genius" would have realized the consequences of running ahead of his supplies over barren countryside in pursuit of an enemy who dictated the time and place of battle. And at every step of the way such a genius would have been thinking of the possible problems of the return journey. Napoleon apparently put such consequences and thoughts out of his mind. One way of interpreting the Russian campaign is to see Napoleon as a general who was so bound by the tactics which had brought him earlier success that he did not have the imagination to change them when they no longer worked. Alternatively, political considerations which are the subject of Chapter 3 may have clouded his military judgment. Either way, his approach to the problem raises doubts about his brilliance as a commander.

Between 1796 and 1808 Napoleon was fortunate in the weight and quality of his opposition. Britain was the only power to offer unflagging resistance in this period, but the resistance was at sea rather than on land. Of the other major states, Austria, Prussia and Russia fought in spells and then were either neutral or in temporary diplomatic agreement with France. Prussia, for example, was neutral between 1795 and 1806. At any given point in time Napoleon was skilful enough to reduce the number of his possible enemies by making friendly gestures or by offering territorial compensation to other countries. In 1799 he allowed the return to Russia of 7000 prisoners of war, and Tsar Paul I responded by withdrawing from the coalition against Napoleon. In 1807, at Tilsit, he reached agreement with Tsar Alexander I by promising that France would not interfere with Russian ambitions in the Balkans. Taken together, all this meant that the French armies were usually able to deal with their enemies one by one. On those occasions when Napoleon was faced by a coalition of two continental powers—in 1805 when he fought the Austrians and the Russians at Austerlitz and in 1806 when it appeared that he would have to deal with a combined Prussian and Russian force—it was to his advantage that he could exercise supreme dictatorial control over French strategy and tactics whereas his enemies were at times uncertain about the methods they should use. Napoleon could act immediately. His enemies had to consult. Perhaps it was this point a French general had in mind when, criticized for his tactics during the First World War, he replied,

Napoleon was not a great general—he only had to fight coalitions.[2]

After 1808 Napoleon could not count on dealing with one power at a time on land. With the British firmly positioned in Portugal, the French armies found themselves fighting Britain, Portugal, Spain and Austria in 1809, Britain, Portugal, Spain and Russia in 1812, and Britain, Austria, Prussia and Russia from 1813. In this new situation Napoleon's generalship was less successful.

The contrast in quality between the opposing land forces in the first half of the Napoleonic period was very marked. The new tactics used by the French have already been mentioned. The enemy armies remained old fashioned. The Prussian army of the time, ". . . slow moving and commanded by aged officers", has been described by Professor Turner:

Its artillery was cumbersome in comparison with the French. The supply system depended on an elaborate organization of convoys and magazines and there was no flexibility of manoeuvre.[3]

It is often said that Prussian forces were moved about on the battlefield as if they were pieces on a chessboard. Certain things could be done;

other things were against the rules. This of course meant that their movements could be predicted. *The Russian Military Code of 1796* laid down similar rigid regulations about troop movements, and reduced the marching rate to 75 paces a minute. This was of great advantage to the French. In 1806 the Prussians, about to face Napoleon, were hoping that the Russian army would arrive in time to help them. The Russians were certainly marching, but at the rate laid down by the Code of 1796. A French cartoon of the time shows the Russian army, mounted on snails and tortoises, "rushing" to the aid of the Prussians.

Marche précipitée de L'armée Russe Volant au secours des prussiens.

Furthermore, the social and political changes brought about in France by the Revolution allowed ordinary men of humble birth to use their talents to gain promotion in the army.

. . . it was fighting qualities which determined the choice between those who succeeded and those who failed. Officers were thus much closer to their men than in the armies of the ancien régime.[2]

The old system of selection still existed in Austria, Prussia and Russia. Promotion in those armies tended to depend on wealth and social position. And to all the French advantages already mentioned there was added another of great importance. As victory followed victory it seemed that French forces were invincible. The morale of the enemy weakened. It was almost as if they expected to be beaten.

All this began to change after 1808. Although the Prussian king would not permit conscription until 1813, a Military Reorganization Committee was set up after the defeat at Jena. On this Committee were military reformers such as Stein and Scharnhorst. In 1807 many

of the senior officers with old fashioned ideas resigned and in 1808 a
Royal Decree changed the basis for promotion in the Prussian army.

*A claim to the position of officer shall from now on be warranted, in peace
time by knowledge and education, in time of war by exceptional bravery
and quickness of perception. . . . All social preference which has hitherto
existed is herewith terminated in the military establishment.*[2]

Changes were also taking place in Russia. Barclay de Tolly took office
as Minister of War in 1810. He placed an emphasis on practical
training rather than on strict drill. On 6 September 1810 he wrote to
his generals:

*. . . the main occupation of a soldier's training should be shooting at a
target.*[4]

He issued instructions for target practice in 1811, and in the same year
his *Code of Infantry Service* demanded that officers

*. . . refrain from dealing out punishment, and take care to explain the
rules with patience, showing what ought to be done and how it ought to be
done.*[4]

In 1812 Major General Kutaisov issued *Rules for the Artillery in Field
Action*, which introduced Russian gunners to the tactics of du Teil.

In Portugal and Spain, Wellington was perfecting infantry
line tactics which could withstand the massive assault of a French
column. Against lines which had shown panic when faced by the onrush
of a column, the French had had notable success. If a line held its
ground, however, and had the courage to delay its heavy volleys until
the last moment, the column was likely to break up and retreat in
confusion. It was such disciplined lines which Wellington created.

*. . . he commanded them to stand up but to hold their fire until the enemy
(was) within 20 or 30 yards of them. . . . At last he gave the word to
fire.*[7]

After the final defeat of Napoleon in 1815, the French writer Bugeaud
described what could happen when one of the columns met a British
line of this kind.

*The English generally occupied well-chosen defensive positions. . . . Soon,
in great haste, without studying the position, without taking time to
examine if there were means to make a flank attack, we marched straight
on (in column) taking the bull by the horns. About a thousand yards from
the English line the men became excited, spoke to one another and hurried
their march; the column began to be a little confused. The English remained
quite silent with ordered arms, and from their steadiness appeared to be a
long red wall. This steadiness invariably produced an effect on the young
soldiers . . . the column began to double, the ranks got into confusion, the*

A STOPPAGE to a STRIDE over the GLOBE

In this British cartoon of 1803, the Giant Napoleon sits astride the Earth, defied only by Britain.

"Ah, who is it dares to interrupt my Progress?" asks Napoleon.

"Why, 'tis I, little Johnny Bull."

In this Russian cartoon of 1812, Napoleon is reduced in size and his flame is being snuffed out by the Russian Giant. (*Crown Copyright, Victoria and Albert Museum.*)

agitation produced a tumult; shots were fired as we advanced. The English line remained still, silent and immovable, with ordered arms, even when we were only three hundred paces distant, and it appeared to ignore the storm about to break. The contrast was striking; in our inmost thoughts, each felt that the enemy was a long time in firing, and that this fire, reserved for so long, would be very unpleasant when it did come. Our ardour cooled. . . . At this moment of intense excitement, the English line shouldered arms; an indescribable feeling rooted many of our men to the spot; they began to fire. The enemy's steady concentrated volleys swept our ranks . . . we turned round . . . then three deafening cheers broke the silence of our opponents; at the third they were on us, pushing our disorganized flight.[2]

In Wellington the opponents of Napoleon now had a commander who was convinced that he would succeed. He felt that "the finger of providence" watched over him. Before taking command in Portugal he was asked by a friend how he felt about meeting the victorious French in battle. He replied,

. . . I am not afraid of them, as everybody else seems to be. . . . I suspect all the continental armies were more than half beaten before the battle was begun. I at least will not be frightened beforehand.[1]

How did Napoleon respond to the new situation as it developed after 1808? He persevered with tactics which had been successful in the past but which were now often unsuitable. Columns which had over-run shaky and undisciplined lines were time and again thrown against lines which did not break. As the opposition improved, Napoleon's inspiration seemed to begin to decline so that

. . . brute force slowly overtook subtlety.[2]

After 1808 the dazzling marches and the skilful use of men were less noticeable.

. . . he lacked the patience for defensive operations.

His reliance on heavy guns increased, and the use of artillery batteries more than doubled. As Wellington saw him slamming cavalry against the solid squares at Waterloo he said,

Damn the fellow, he is a mere pounder after all.[7]

And the Emperor's judgment, on the decline for some time, reached a low point on the eve of Waterloo. Marshal Soult, having had experience of Wellington, was explaining some of the difficulties which lay ahead. Napoleon interrupted,

Because you have been defeated by Wellington, you think him a great general. I tell you that Wellington is a bad general, that the English are bad troops and that this will be a picnic.[6]

The Beginning

"What I have done so far is nothing. I am only at the beginning of the course I must run. . . . The nation must have a chief, and a chief rendered illustrious by glory."
(*Napoleon, 1797*)

And The End

"In the morning the Emperor had asked at least twenty times whether he might be allowed to have some coffee. But every time the answer had been, 'No, Sire.'

'Won't the doctors allow me just a spoonful?'

'No, Sire, not at present.'

What thoughts sprang to mind at the sight of so great a change! Tears came to my eyes, as I looked at this man, formerly so terrifying, who had commanded so proudly . . . now reduced to begging for a spoonful of coffee, asking permission, obedient as a child, asking permission again and again without obtaining it."
(*Bertrand, 26 April 1821*)

Contrasting views of Napoleon crossing
the Alps on his Second Italian Campaign.
In the painting by David (right) the
First Consul is splendid and majestic; in
the painting by Delaroche (above),
Napoleon is a slight and huddled figure
on a mule. Which image belongs to the
Legend and which to reality?

In yet other respects Napoleon's generalship has been criticized. Many historians have argued that he did not give his marshals enough freedom to make their own decisions during a campaign. This is perhaps unfair. As we have seen, Napoleon's armies were often divided into separate units when they were on the march. The officers commanding each unit would naturally receive orders from Bonaparte on the direction and speed of their march so that he could have some idea of their location at any particular time. It was not to be expected that the commanding general would allow his subordinates to march where they liked or at a pace of their own choice. The effectiveness of the whole army depended upon the co-operation of each unit. However, in the course of a march, circumstances might demand that a general had to make a quick decision. His unit, for example, might come under a sudden and unexpected attack. He would have to respond as he thought fit. He could not send off a messenger and *wait* until he returned with the Chief's views. Furthermore, in the heat of battle there were many occasions when generals and marshals were not in contact with Napoleon. At such times they had to make their own decisions. But this is not the whole story. In another sense Napoleon *did* severely limit the initiative of his generals. And he did so in two different ways.

There is evidence to show that Napoleon stubbornly insisted that any order given by him should be carried out to the letter. Now it is natural that a commander-in-chief should wish that his orders be obeyed. An army could hardly be successful if the leader's instructions were ignored. But in days when the distances, often great, between units or armies had to be covered either on foot or on horseback, an order could be received long after the set of circumstances to which it applied had passed. Was it wise then of Napoleon to create the impression that his orders had to be carried out, even if they were no longer appropriate? He attempted to conduct the war in Portugal and Spain by remote control. While campaigning in central or eastern Europe he would

> . . . *send orders to Spain (which) were usually hopelessly out of date and inapplicable to a changing situation.*

Yet he expected the orders to be obeyed. In April 1804 Napoleon wrote to Rear Admiral Decrés, Minister for the Navy:

> *I am signing a decree to-day about naval construction. I will listen to no objection. . . . I shall not regard any excuse as valid.*[8]

Some would no doubt argue that this is the way to get work done. If a commander takes a strong line with his subordinates they may try to perform miracles. But when Napoleon said, ". . . I shall not regard any excuse as valid", he meant that no matter how reasonable the objections were he would not accept them. In other words, if an order to do the impossible was not carried out, the subordinate had failed. In a dispatch dated 8 October 1809 to General de Wrede, the commander of his Bavarian allies, Napoleon wrote:

I will have no one objecting to me with "if" or "but" or "because".[5]

This stubbornness sometimes had disastrous results. An incident at Boulogne in July 1804 demonstrates his belief that his orders were never open to challenge.

One morning [at Boulogne] the Emperor signified his intention of reviewing the fleet, and gave orders for the ships to take up . . . positions, as the review was to be held right out at sea. [Then] he went out for his usual ride. . . . Everyone knew that the Emperor's wish was law, and, in his absence, Admiral Bruix was informed of it. He coolly replied that he was really very sorry, but that there could be no review that day. Consequently, not a vessel budged.

On coming back, the Emperor . . . was told of the Admiral's reply. . . . Stamping his foot violently, he sent for the Admiral. . . . "How is it, Admiral," said the Emperor, "that you have not carried out my instructions?"

"Sire," replied Bruix, respectfully but firmly, "an awful storm is brewing; Your Majesty can see that as well as I can. Does Your Majesty wish thus uselessly to imperil the lives of so many brave fellows?"

"Sir," exclaimed the Emperor, with increasing irritation, "I gave an order. *Once more I ask, how is it you did not execute it? I alone am responsible for the consequences.* Obey!"

"Sire, I shall not *obey."*

"Monsieur, you are an insolent fellow!"

And the Emperor, who still had his riding-whip in his hand, advanced towards the Admiral with a threatening gesture. Admiral Bruix, stepping back, gripped his sword-hilt.

"Have a care, Sire," said he, turning deadly pale.

All the onlookers grew cold with fear. For some time, with an arm uplifted, the Emperor stood motionless, glaring at the Admiral, who unflinchingly maintained his grim attitude. At last the Emperor flung away his whip, and M. Bruix relinquished his grasp of his sword-hilt as . . . he silently awaited the result of so terrible a scene.

"Vice-Admiral Magon," said the Emperor, "you will at once execute the movement which I ordered. As for you, sir," he continued,

turning to Admiral Bruix, "you will leave Boulogne in twenty-four hours and withdraw to Holland. . . ."

The Vice-Admiral proceeded to carry out the Emperor's instructions. Yet scarcely had the first dispositions been taken than the sea assumed a fearful aspect. . . . Thunder boomed incessantly in angry peals, and there came a great wind, which threw the vessels into grievous disorder. . . . In short, that which the Admiral foresaw occurred, and a most appalling tempest dispersed all the war-ships in such a way that their destruction seemed assured.[8]

The outcome of Napoleon's often unreasonable attitude to his orders was that some generals were unwilling to risk his disfavour by failing to carry them out, even if obedience could have unfortunate results. At Waterloo, Marshal Grouchy had been ordered *to follow* Wellington's Prussian ally, Blücher. This is precisely what he did. A more enterprising general might have gone beyond his orders and attempted to get between Blücher and Wellington, but since Napoleon had thought that the Prussians were moving east, and *away* from Wellington, the order had been to follow. As a result, Grouchy was always behind Blücher, and the Prussians were able to join up with Wellington to inflict final defeat on the French. Grouchy, blamed for Napoleon's failure at Waterloo, spoke the following words in his own defence:

Inspiration in war is appropriate only to the commander-in-chief, and his lieutenants must confine themselves to executing orders.[2]

If Grouchy ". . . took refuge in a literal obedience to orders . . ." it was at least partly because Napoleon had encouraged the habit.

The second way in which Bonaparte limited the initiative of his subordinates stems from the fact that he

. . . never shared with anyone the responsibility for formulating strategic conceptions and issuing general orders.[9]

It has been seen that this was something of an advantage when the French were fighting coalitions. On the other hand it meant that

. . . there existed no necessity for an abundance of truly capable men.

The consequences have been described by Professor Lefebvre:

Frequently, as the theatres of war increased, Napoleon's absence betrayed the fact that few of his lieutenants were fit to command-in-chief . . . he failed . . . in forming his High Command . . . to provide officers with [training] in grand strategy.[9]

In 1806 Napoleon wrote to Marshal Berthier:

Adhere strictly to the commands which I give you. I alone know what I have to do.[9]

This unwillingness to share responsibility, to train his leading officers in the skills of high command, was noticed by Baron Meneval, Bonaparte's secretary from 1802 to 1813:

> *If any regret can be expressed . . . it is that the unceasing activity of the finest intellect which has ever been granted to a human being, should have accustomed his agents to await his inspiration and to distrust themselves; and that in consequence, so many men of talent should have found themselves paralysed and taken by surprise in moments of danger.*[8]

The Legend never takes account of such reality because it did not examine the weaknesses in Napoleon's style of command.

For all his ability to appreciate the value of new methods, Napoleon had blind spots.

> *. . . In 1800 [he] disbanded the French Balloon Unit, which had rendered notable service in the Belgian campaign of 1794 and had also been employed in Germany by the French Army of the Rhine. For this decision Napoleon was to pay dearly, for aerial reconnaissance would have helped him immeasurably at . . . Waterloo.*[3]

The point about aerial reconnaissance is important. When we look at a diagram of a battlefield it is as if we were having an aerial view of events. We are "looking down" on the movement of troops. If a French Balloon Unit had been observing the Battle of Waterloo between 16–18 June 1815 it would have been looking down on the three main stages of the battle in much the same way that we look down on the diagram opposite.

Stage 1: On 16 June Marshal Ney engaged Wellington's forces at Quatre Bras and Napoleon fought Blücher's Prussians at Ligny. General d'Erlon was located between Quatre Bras and Ligny, but ". . . his corps of 20,000 men spent 16 June wandering between two battles and failing to fire a shot in either".

Stage 2: Believing that Blücher would retreat east, it was Napoleon's hope that by sending Marshal Grouchy with 32,000 men in the direction of Liège the Prussians would be intercepted and so be unable to reinforce Wellington.

Stage 3: Wellington's forces withdrew to Mont St Jean, pursued by Napoleon and the French forces west of Ligny. The decisive battle was fought on 18 June. Blücher was able to link up with Wellington, but Grouchy's forces did not reach the final battlefield.

If a French Balloon Unit had been observing the lay-out and movement of troops, vital information could have been passed to Napoleon. All generals make mistakes, and Napoleon was no exception. The Legend does not take account of this, however, and

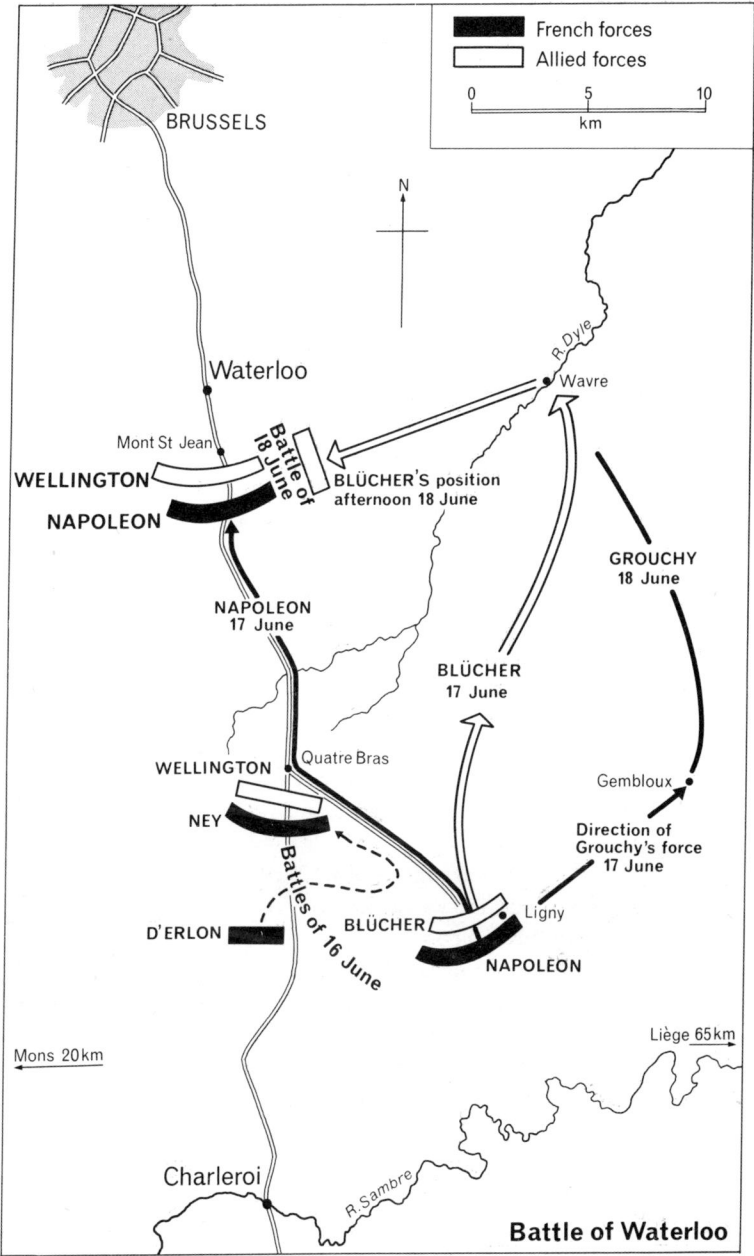

Battle of Waterloo

overlooks the fact that in disbanding the Balloon Unit he showed that he could at times lack imagination and farsightedness.

Finally, the reality of one of Bonaparte's greatest "victories" shows how history enacted and history remembered can be very different things. The story of the Battle of Marengo (1800) was distorted to support the Legend. Truth was twisted in order to present contemporaries and posterity with the impression of a great personal triumph in which everything was foreseen and nothing went seriously wrong from Napoleon's point of view.

On 13 June 1800, Bonaparte and Melas, the Austrian commander, prepared for battle on the Plain of Marengo, with just over 30,000 men apiece. When the Austrians withdrew to what was for them a better defensive position, Napoleon thought that they were in full retreat. He therefore sent two divisions, totalling 8800 men, one under Desaix and the other under Lapoype to cut them off. But then, at 9.00 a.m. on 14 June, Melas attacked and Napoleon was left with about 23,000 men and 20 artillery pieces against a much stronger enemy supported by 100 cannon. However, he still felt that the attack was a trick to conceal an Austrian retreat and so he sent a message to Desaix instructing him to continue his march at speed *away from Marengo*. At midday, with no reserves left, and with ammunition running low, Napoleon realized that a mistake had been made. Desperate messages were sent off, recalling Desaix and Lapoype. The latter was too far away, but Desaix was able to turn back in time simply because a swollen river had luckily delayed him. The arrival of Desaix and his men between 4.00 p.m. and 5.00 p.m. swung the battle in favour of the French.

The story of Marengo was falsified in four separate stages. *The Bulletin* of 15 June 1800 awarded some credit to Desaix, but gave the impression that Napoleon was always in firm control of the battle. Then in 1803 Bonaparte ordered that a new account be written. The story was now that Desaix had been detached for the same reason that Serurier had been detached at Castiglione—that is, to be in a position to move up to the main battle area at short notice. In 1805 Napoleon revisited Marengo, refought the battle in his mind, and ordered yet another account. And then, on St Helena, further embellishments were added so that

> Napoleon could conclude with an account of Marengo which conceals that he had lost the battle, and slides almost without mention over Desaix who had come to his rescue. It is a fitting end to a narrative which is . . . full of lies.[10]

So far as his military activities were concerned, the Napoleon of the Legend is not the Napoleon of reality. He was much less than the superman who knew and did all. If his successes were great so too were his failures. And yet, if he was not always ". . . a great master of war", he was certainly no ordinary commander. "There never was a general in whose presence it was more dangerous to make a false step", wrote Wellington, and if the Duke is regarded as a hero in British military history it is probably because he defeated a giant.

---

[1]*Big Battalions: The Napoleonic Legacy* by John Terraine (HISTORY TODAY, June 1962); [2]*NCMH* Volume IX; [3]*Napoleon and Europe* by L. C. F. Turner (WARNE); [4]*Borodino and the War of 1812* by Christopher Duffy (SPHERE); [5]*Napoleon Bonaparte* letters translated by J. M. Thompson (DENT); [6]*The Great Duke* by A. Bryant (COLLINS); [7]*The Great Duke* by Elizabeth Longford (SUNDAY TIMES MAGAZINE, 13 April 1969); [8]*Napoleon: Great Lives Observed* ed. M.. Hutt (PRENTICE-HALL); [9]*Napoleon* Volume 1 by G. Lefebvre (ROUTLEDGE & KEGAN PAUL); [10]*Europe: Grandeur and Decline* by A. J. P. Taylor (PENGUIN).

3

All in Self-defence

apoleon ruled France as First Consul from December 1799 to April 1804, and as Emperor from May 1804 to April 1814. In all that time, France was at peace for less than two years. Why was war such a feature of the Napoleonic period? If we are to believe the Legend, it was no fault of the great man. Glory and conquest never entered into Napoleon's calculations. Peace was his only thought.

> *Throughout his whole reign,* wrote Albert Vandal, *Napoleon pursued one unchanging objective in his foreign policy . . . the peace of the world.*[1]

But he was forced to fight, simply because his enemies, and Britain in particular, would not permit him to retain, without war, the natural frontiers won by the Revolutionary governments. A French state bounded by the Rhine and the Alps in the north and east could not be tolerated by the other powers. In refusing to surrender the natural frontiers Napoleon became a prisoner of circumstances. He did not build the road along which he had to travel.

In this version of events, Bonaparte is an attractive figure. There is something heroic, even tragic, about the man who takes up the sword reluctantly, goes to war unwillingly, and yet triumphs. It is, however, a version which leaves many questions unanswered. Were all the provocations on the allied side? Did Napoleon recognize any limits to the defence of the natural frontiers; for example, where was such a defence to end; was it on the Rhine and at the Alps, or ten, fifty, one hundred, two or three hundred kilometres east and south of those positions? Were there no opportunities to end the wars and yet retain the frontiers? And what did Napoleon mean by a "just and lasting peace"? It is also a version which ignores other explanations for the wars of the period. No account is taken of Napoleon's personality. No attempt is made to link his foreign policy with his problems as a domestic ruler. Legends are usually simple and uncomplicated; this is not often the case with real human activity.

Of one thing we can be sure. The war which was in progress when he took control of France in 1799 was not his direct responsibility. He inherited it. Austria, Britain and Russia had formed a coalition against France in 1798. Russia withdrew in December 1800, Austria made peace at Lunéville in January 1801, and Britain came to terms with France at Amiens in March 1802. After this time the issues become clouded. It is true that it was Britain which reopened direct hostilities in the summer of 1803; it is also true that Russia allied with Britain in April 1805 and that Austria joined the coalition in August of the same year. Stated in this way, without any qualification, it seems that the Legend has some merit. Is it not clear that the other powers simply refused to leave France in peace? If the question is clear-cut this is not so with the answer.

Britain did not respect the Treaty of Amiens in its entirety. Neither did Napoleon. Furthermore, it could be said that while both failed to respect the full letter of the Peace, it was France which most notably failed to respect its spirit. Two provisions of the negotiations had been that France evacuate troops from Holland and Britain give up possession of Malta. Neither was fulfilled. This was cause enough for troubled relationships between the two countries, but the situation was made much worse by other moves on Napoleon's part. It appeared that France had ambitions in the East. In August 1802 Napoleon sent General Sebastiani on a mission to Egypt. On his return in January 1803 a report was published in the government's official newspaper, *Le Moniteur*. It contained the significant comment:

> . . . *six thousand men would suffice to reconquer Egypt.*[2]

Another representative, on a similar political mission, was sent to India in March 1803. There was other evidence which suggested that Napoleon had far reaching ambitions. In September 1802 Piedmont, in north-west Italy, was annexed by France and in October of the same year French troops moved into the neighbouring province of Parma. This was followed by the closure of the ports of Napoleon's vassal Italian states to British commerce. In September 1802 the French carried through a military intervention in Switzerland. *All this during a period of peace.* Are we to see here a man solely concerned with the natural frontiers? Are we to consider that Napoleon's activities were in no way provocative? If Britain was worried, so too was Russia. French encroachments in the Mediterranean had to be carefully watched. And Austria was deeply concerned by the way in which Bonaparte broke the terms of the Treaty of Lunéville. The Cisalpine and Ligurian Republics were supposed to remain independent.

Napoleon swept this provision aside when in May 1805 the first became the Kingdom of Italy with himself as its monarch and in June the second was annexed by France.

It is important, of course, to ask why the other powers took exception to Napoleon's moves. No one would be foolish enough to argue that they were totally selfless in their attitudes. Apart from thinking of their own safety they also thought of their own ambitions. Like Napoleon, they had ideas about where power should and should not lie. Bonaparte did not invent annexations. Austria and Russia had helped to carve up Poland in the second half of the eighteenth century. Britain was not backward in her empire building. And while showing grave concern about the balance of power on the continent—being constantly watchful against the possibility that one power might dominate Europe—Britain did not mind that she had almost complete control of the sea. After all ". . . in her eyes God had created the oceans for the English". It is probably true to say, then, that

the conflict between Bonaparte and England was in reality a clash between two imperialisms.[2]

The intention, therefore, is not to lay all the guilt on Napoleon and reveal Austria, Britain and Russia as innocents. Yet can any doubt remain that a look at both sides of the argument makes suspect the claim that Napoleon's wars were always fought in self-defence, that he never offered provocation? If this is true of events during 1801–05, how much more so of the 1808–12 period. Were the French invasions of Spain and Portugal, then Russia, simply acts of self-defence? And what of the return from Elba in March 1815? For almost a year Napoleon had lived in exile on the Mediterranean island. Why did he return? Was it to reclaim the natural frontiers, or was there a more selfish motive in his mind? When the allied powers gathered for the final battle in 1815 were they the aggressors?

It was to be expected that Napoleon would defend the natural frontiers. Yet when his methods are examined it is difficult to avoid the suspicion that this was not his only aim. Consider this model:

The shaded area represents the territory to be defended. It would be possible to defend the frontiers by building extensive fortifications and establishing large garrisons, but if enemies launched an attack they could break through immediately into the shaded area. What is needed is a "buffer" between the enemy and the home territory. Sound strategy demands that area 2 be taken over to act as such a buffer. Of course, the defenders may then want a "buffer for the buffer", and so on, with the result that areas 3, 4, 5, 6, etc., are taken over. *But if this happens, the original frontiers are left further and further behind.* Where then does the defence of the frontiers end and European conquest begin?

It is reasonable to suppose that some territory north and east of the Rhine and east and south of the Alps was necessary to protect the natural frontiers. The extent of the territory either directly or indirectly controlled by France was so great, however, that we are bound to ask if Napoleon's policy was aggressive rather than defensive. Was it necessary to control the whole of Italy, large areas on the east coast of the Adriatic, the Duchy of Warsaw, and 500 kilometres east of the Rhine, in order to defend the natural frontiers? Edouard Driault provided one answer to such a question:

> . . . *he was less concerned to safeguard France's security behind her natural frontiers than to conquer the Empire for himself.*[1]

Of course, this is not the last word on the matter. But note that Driault struck a balance. He did not suggest that Napoleon had absolutely no concern for the frontiers. Balance is a word quite foreign to the Legend.

The message from St Helena was that Napoleon's "sole aim was to arrive at a just and lasting peace". Peace is of course always the final aim in war, but this in itself means nothing. It is the terms of peace which count. Napoleon was well aware of this. In a letter to his brother Joseph, dated 13 December 1805, he wrote:

> *The word "peace" means nothing.* It is a particular kind of peace we want—*peace with glory.*[3]

The particular kind of peace which would have been acceptable to the other powers—a peace based on concessions from both sides—was clearly not the kind of peace desired by Napoleon.

> *No mind was ever less capable of understanding the necessity of compromise.*[1]

Bonaparte had an opportunity to make peace in 1813–14 and still retain the natural frontiers. We can never be absolutely certain why he rejected the opportunity, but at least part of the problem was that he would have been required to give up some of his conquests.

In June 1813, Austrian and Russian representatives met to draw up terms which would be offered to France. It was decided that if Napoleon showed himself prepared to make concessions, he could retain the frontiers. If he refused the offer and continued the war, the frontiers would be lost. Following this, either Napoleon or his Foreign Minister, Caulaincourt, met with Metternich of Austria in negotiations at Dresden and Prague. The proposals laid before the French were:

1. Prussia to regain her Polish territory.

2. France to give up her protectorate of the Confederation of the Rhine.

3. France to give up the coastal towns of northern Germany, in the region of Denmark.

4. France to return Illyria (east coast of Adriatic) to Austria.

In August 1813, Caulaincourt addressed the following letter to his master:

No doubt your Majesty will see in this ultimatum some sacrifice of pride, but there will be no real sacrifice for France. . . . I beseech you, Sire, let all the chances of war be weighed in the balance with peace; have regard to the irritation in men's hearts, France's fatigue, her noble devotion, the sacrifices she made after the Russian disaster; listen to the prayers of this same France for peace. . . .[1]

Napoleon would not bend. In Cobban's view,

moderation had long since ceased to be possible for him.[4]

In fairness it must be said that, when the allies invaded France in 1814, Napoleon did attempt to negotiate on the retention of the natural frontiers and no more. It was too late, of course, and too much like the last desperate throw of the gambler. At this point Caulaincourt wrote:

The cause of our disappointments is in the refusal to make timely concessions, and it will end by ruining us completely.[1]

Overlooking evidence which would have been inconvenient, the Legend also ignores explanations which would have been unfavourable to Napoleon. Why, for example, was no attempt made to explore the man's personality as a means of understanding why he campaigned throughout Europe for eighteen years? As Napoleon speaks for himself, ask if the words are those of a man of restraint and moderation.

In conversation with Las Cases, 1815

It was on the evening after Lodi (1796) that I realized I was a superior being and conceived the ambition of performing great things, which hitherto had filled my thoughts only as fantastic dreams.[5]

Letter to brother Joseph, August 1795
Personally, I hardly care what happens to me. . . . My permanent
state of mind is that of a soldier on the eve of battle. . . . *This
attitude is a natural tendency produced . . .* by the habit of running
risks.[3]

To Joseph, 1804
I believe I am destined to change the face of the world.[5]

*Death is nothing, but to live defeated and without glory is to die every
day.*[2]

This was a man who ". . . felt himself strong enough to overcome all
obstacles", who ". . . believed that there was nothing personally
impossible for him". A personality, fulfilling itself, in the words of
Gabriel Hanotaux, in

*this enjoyment of action . . . this hunt for an ever more exalted . . . prey.
. . . This excitement . . . in the mastering . . . of the future of the
world. . . .*[1]

Here was ". . . a force seeking to expand and for which the world was
no more than an occasion for acting dangerously".

It is not difficult to see this personality, allied to undoubted
military skill, becoming trapped in his own legend of invincibility.
He dropped a hint that this might be so when, during his last campaign,
he wrote:

I had no longer within me the feeling of certain success.[5]

On and ever on he went until the final impossibility remained an
impossibility. But before this point was reached, immoderation
increased with every success. When searching for the motives behind
his activities it may well be true that ". . . in the last resort we must
return to his ambition".

There is yet another argument of which the Legend takes no
note. Put in the form of a question it is: To what extent was war
necessary to maintain his position in France? Writing in 1866, of
Bonaparte's nephew, Napoleon III, Bismark made an excellent
analysis of the problems facing a dictatorship which is not founded on
tradition.

*A king of Prussia can make mistakes, can suffer misfortune and even
humiliation, but the old loyalty remains. The adventurer on the throne
possesses no such heritage of confidence. He must always produce an effect.
His safety depends on his personal prestige, and to enhance it sensations
must follow each other in rapid succession.*[6]

There is no doubt that Napoleon appreciated the difficulties of his position. In 1799, taking his first steps as ruler, he commented,

In Paris nothing is ever remembered for long. If I remain doing nothing for long, I am lost.

In a remarkable conversation with a member of his Council of State in 1802, Napoleon used words very close to those of Bismark.

. . . Are military victories no longer necessary for creating an impression on the public and keeping a hold on the domestic front? Remember that a First Consul is not like those kings appointed by the Grace of God, who look upon their states as their inheritance. They are assisted in their rule by old habits of thought. . . . The French government today is quite unlike any other . . . it has to resort to actions which create a great impression, and consequently it resorted to war. . . . My government must be the foremost [in all Europe]; otherwise it will be destroyed.

Bonaparte held to his view consistently. Chaptal recorded Napoleon's comments on the subject in 1812:

France does not really understand the situation I am in . . . I can only keep myself there by using force. . . . The moment I cease to be feared my Empire will collapse. . . . The king who comes of an ancient line can ignore things which I, on the contrary, have to take seriously. . . . For me there is always at stake . . . my very existence. . . . At home, as abroad, I reign because of the fear I inspire; and if I changed my system I should soon be dethroned.

It is perhaps only in this last sense that the Legend touches reality, although unwittingly. When the phrase "self-defence" is used it is "the defence of France" which is meant. With Napoleon the wars were to some extent *in his own defence*. In most other respects Legend and reality again drift apart. It was not to be expected that Napoleon could spread his influence over Europe without producing responses from the other powers. He chose to regard such responses as unwarranted aggression, and so could claim that his wars were in defence of France. Yet his enemies could argue, with some justification, that they were fighting for survival. Those insights into his personality provided by his own words hint at a man who was more likely to adopt aggressive than defensive postures.

---

[1] *Napoleon: For and Against* by P. Geyl (CAPE); [2] *Napoleon* Volume 1 by G. Lefebvre (ROUTLEDGE & KEGAN PAUL); [3] *Napoleon Bonaparte* letters translated by J. M. Thompson (DENT); [4] *A History of Modern France* Volume 2 by A. Cobban (PENGUIN); [5] *NCMH* Volume IX; [6] *Bismarck* by A. J. P. Taylor (HAMISH HAMILTON).

4

I am the Revolution

$\mathcal{L}$ ooking back from St Helena, Napoleon saw his reign as "the embodiment of the Revolution". He and the great event could not be separated. They were one and the same thing. Jules Michelet, on the other hand, regarded him as "the betrayer of the Revolution". In judging between those two opposing views we are faced with a problem more complex than any so far tackled. The difficulty lies in the fact that there was no "one thing", no uniform episode, which we can call "The French Revolution". All that can be said is that there was a "Revolutionary period" in France, beginning just before 1789 and lasting for five or six years. Within this period there were a number of different revolutionary phases, and there were so many changes of direction and emphasis, that each phase was quite distinct in a number of ways from the others. If the validity of Napoleon's words, "*I am the Revolution*," is to be tested at all, we must be absolutely sure of the particular phase to which we are referring. For it may be that in relation to one phase Napoleon was not, whereas in relation to another he was, "the embodiment of the Revolution". It may even be that there are similarities as well as divergences between the work of Napoleon and the work of all phases of the period. And it is possible that there is more room for differences of opinion on this than on any other aspect of the Legend.

Despite the difficulties, two firm statements can be made immediately. In one sense Napoleon embodied all the phases of the Revolution. In yet another he ran counter to all.

Napoleon rose to fame in the service of the Revolutionary governments. His career was linked in two vital ways to the course of the Revolution. He profited from the principles laid down in Article VI of the *Declaration of the Rights of Man and of the Citizen*, adopted by the National Assembly on 27 August 1789:

Law is the expression of the General Will. . . . All citizens, being equal before it, are equally admissible to all public offices, positions, and

> *employments, according to their capacity, and without other distinction other than that of virtues and talents,*

and also from the fact that approximately 8000 army officers left France after 1789 because they were out of sympathy with what was happening. Displaying talent at a time when it was in short supply, Napoleon achieved rapid promotion. The First Lieutenant of 1791 became the Captain of 1792. In 1793 he was raised to acting Lieutenant Colonel in command of artillery at Toulon, and played a large part in the defeat of British forces which had landed at the port. As a reward for this service he became a Brigadier General. For his part in putting down a royalist rising in Paris in October 1795 he was raised to Major General, and then given supreme command of the Army of Italy in March 1796. There is a great deal of merit in Albert Sorel's assessment that

> *. . . it was the French Revolution . . . those growing pains of France, these enthusiastic armies, that is what has made Bonaparte, through that he is everything; without it, in spite of his genius, he would be nothing but a prodigious and powerless individual.*[1]

On the other hand, one of the things thrown aside by the Revolutionaries was the notion of Divine Right as a support for authority. It did not re-emerge in any guise or at any time between 1790 and 1799. Authority came from the people, not from God. The Napoleonic years were quite different in this respect. *The Seventh Lesson of the Imperial Catechism*, published in 1806 for use in schools and pulpits, indicates Napoleon's return to the idea of Divine Right

> *Q: What are the duties of Christians with respect to the princes who govern them, and what are in particular our duties toward Napoleon I, our Emperor?*
>
> *A: . . . love, respect, obedience, fidelity, military service, tributes ordered for the preservation and defence of the Empire and of his throne; we also owe him fervent prayers for his safety and for the spiritual and temporal prosperity of the State.*
>
> *Q: Why do we have these duties towards our Emperor?*
>
> *A: First, because by bountifully bestowing talents on our Emperor both in peace and war, God has established him as our sovereign and has made him the minister of His power and His image on earth. To honour and serve our Emperor is therefore to honour and serve God himself.*
>
> *Q: Are there not special motives which must attach us more strongly to Napoleon, our Emperor?*
>
> *A: Yes: for he is the one whom God has given us in difficult times to re-establish the public worship of the holy religion of our fathers and to*

Le Soutien de la France

A typical example of Napoleonic art. Revolutionary extremism (bottom
right), with the knife of faction between its teeth, and symbols of slavery in
its hands, has led France to the edge of the abyss, into which Ignorance (left)
tries to pull her. Bonaparte comes to the rescue and turns her back towards
Justice, Unity, Peace and Plenty.

"With one bold leap of the imagination he lifted himself up to Charlemange."
(Geyl) One explanation of Napoleonic warfare is that it served his dream of
Imperial grandeur. This portrait, painted by Ingres in 1806, resembles
ninth century portraits of Charlemange.

be the protector of it. He has re-established and maintained public order by his profound and active wisdom; he defends the State with his powerful arm; he has become the Lord's anointed through the consecration which he received from the pontifical sovereign, head of the universal church.

Q: What must one think of those who may fail in their duty towards our Emperor?

A: According to the apostle Paul, they would resist the established order of God himself and would be worthy of eternal damnation.

Q: Do the duties towards our Emperor bind us equally towards his successors?

A: Yes, undoubtedly; for we read in the holy scripture that God, Lord of Heaven and earth . . . gives empires not only to one person in particular, but also to his family.

In 1809 Napoleon declared, "We hold OUR throne from GOD, and WE are accountable to him alone for OUR actions." Metternich recalled a conversation he had with Bonaparte in 1810.

He was also much impressed with the idea of deriving the origin of supreme authority from the Divinity. . . . He said it is a fine custom . . . power comes from God, and it is that alone which places it beyond the attacks of men . . .[2]

In this Napoleon cannot be seen as the embodiment of the Revolution.

The proclamation to the nation, announcing the new Constitution of 1799, contained the words:

Citizens, the Revolution is established on the principles with which it began. It is complete.[3]

Was Napoleon's system of government really similar to that set up in France after 1789? In the early years of the Revolutionary period the principle of effective representative government was in the forefront of men's minds. When the States-General met in 1789 it was doing so for the first time in 175 years. It was felt that most of the problems of France stemmed from the fact that the people had not had a say in the running of the country. The following articles come from the *List of Grievances and Complaints of the Members of the Third Estate of Versailles*, published on the eve of the Revolution:

1. The power of making laws resides in the King and the nation.

2. The nation being too numerous for a personal exercise of this right, has confided its trust to representatives freely chosen from all classes of citizens. . . .

6. . . . the nation may not be deprived of that portion of legislation which is its due. . . .[4]

When Sieyes published his pamphlet, *What is the Third Estate?*, at the end of 1788, it was clear that the people were claiming a major say in government.

> *The plan of this pamphlet is simple. We have three questions to ask:*
> *1st: What is the Third Estate?* **Everything**
> *2nd: What has it been heretofore?* **Nothing**
> *3rd: What does it demand?* **To become something**
> *. . . The Third Estate alone, they say, cannot constitute the States-General. Well, so much the better. It will form a National Assembly.*

And Article III of the *Declaration of the Rights of Man and of the Citizen* began:

> *The principle of sovereignty emanates essentially from the nation.*

It was not surprising, therefore, that the Constitution of 1791 was weighted heavily in favour of the legislature, or that there was a strict separation of powers. In the early years politicians insisted that any increase in the power of the executive side of government was a source of peril to the Revolution. The voice of the people, as represented in the legislature, had to be heard. And what it commanded was law.

The Napoleonic system was vastly different. "Power is my mistress," said Bonaparte, "I love it as a musician loves his violin; I love it as an artist." As one historian put it, Napoleon might have added, "The artist dare not lend his violin, and least of all to an incompetent player. . . ." The great man had no intention of sharing power, least of all with the people.

In Napoleon's political system, at central government level, the executive authority first dominated, then by-passed, the legislature. "No more striking contrast with the Revolutionary Assemblies could have been invented." It is difficult to disagree with the comment that

> *it was not a framework for the kind of society that the idealistic liberals of 1789 had imagined themselves to be inaugurating. . . .*[5]

The case is sometimes made that Napoleon's Government did not differ all that much from the system in operation during the Reign of Terror. It is true that for almost a year in the period 1793–94 the Committee of Public Safety, dominated by Robespierre and St Just, held executive authority and also exercised a great deal of control over the legislature in the shape of the Convention. But this control was never formal, it was not written into the Constitution, and had to be won by the personality and standing of the leaders of the Committee. In the end it was the Convention which broke free and brought about the fall of Robespierre. The similarities between Napoleon's system

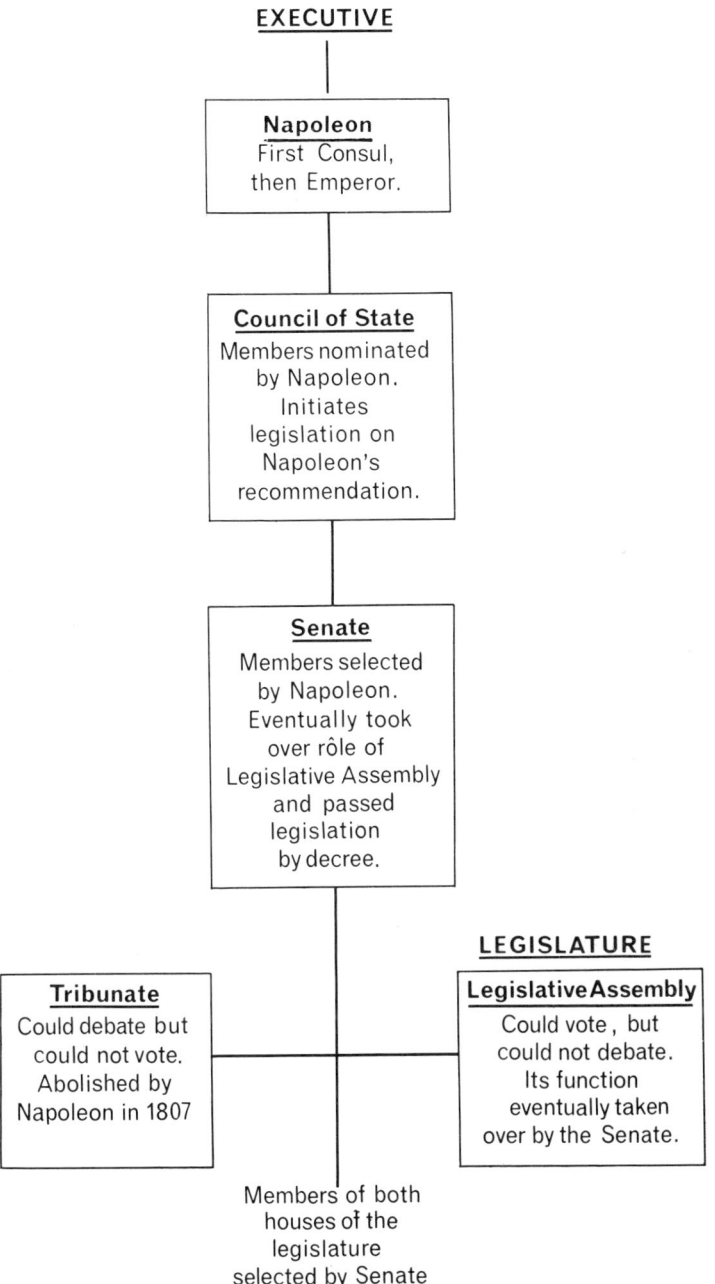

EXECUTIVE

Napoleon
First Consul,
then Emperor.

Council of State
Members nominated
by Napoleon.
Initiates
legislation on
Napoleon's
recommendation.

Senate
Members selected
by Napoleon.
Eventually took
over rôle of
Legislative Assembly
and passed
legislation
by decree.

LEGISLATURE

Tribunate
Could debate but
could not vote.
Abolished by
Napoleon in 1807

Legislative Assembly
Could vote, but
could not debate.
Its function
eventually taken
over by the Senate.

Members of both
houses of the
legislature
selected by Senate
from national lists.

and the so-called "Jacobin Dictatorship" are not as significant as the contrasts, at least so far as central government is concerned. It would have been more appropriate had Napoleon said, "L'état c'est moi" rather than "*I am the Revolution*". And this of course would have brought him closer to Louis XIV than to the Revolutionary period.

The situation is not just so clear-cut when we examine local government. In the first two years after 1789 the elaborate, centralized structure for local government built up during the *ancien régime* was dismantled. Regions, districts and towns were given control of their own affairs. The 83 Départements of France were administered by locally elected committees, and in roughly 36,000 communes the mayors and councillors were elected by local citizens. There was always a possibility under such a system that the local bodies would prove insubordinate to the central authorities. This was a possibility which Napoleon refused to tolerate. His local government law of February 1800 centralized administration throughout France. The Départements were retained, but were divided into "arrondissements". Over each Département was set a Prefect, over each arrondissement a sub-Prefect. Those officials were appointed by the central government, in effect by Napoleon. Mayors of communes were no longer elected by the inhabitants. In communes of less than 5000 persons the Mayor was chosen by the Prefect, and in communes of more than 5000 persons, by Napoleon: ". . . the result was practical efficiency at the cost of local initiative."

Again it seems that Napoleonic policy was against the work of the Revolution. But here a qualification is valid. During the Reign of Terror when it was felt that France was threatened by internal as well as external enemies, the Committee of General Security re-imposed central authority on local government. "Representatives on Mission", with broad powers, were sent out into the districts to ensure that national policy was being carried out. So far as local government is concerned, Napoleon's claim is not entirely without foundation.

One of the great emotive slogans of the Revolution was "Liberty, Equality, Fraternity". Inequality had been a feature of the *ancien régime*, most obvious of all being inequality of taxation and of opportunity. After 1789, privilege was abolished and a new principle introduced,

La carrière ouverte aux talens.

Natural and social inequality remained, of course, but *legal* inequality was thrown over, as indicated by Article VI of the *Declaration of Rights* which has already been quoted. There is general agreement that with regard to equality, "Bonaparte . . . respected the great social achievements of the Revolution. . . ." He was fond of remarking, with justification,

I made most of my generals de la boue (out of mud)[2]

Of his Marshals, Masséna was the son of a wine merchant, Ney of a cooper, Murat of a publican, Lannes of an ostler, and Augereau of a stonemason. When he was looking for talent he was prepared to accept it wherever it was to be found. Before 1789, Barnave, who was to play a leading part in the Revolutionary period protested against privilege when he cried,

The road is blocked in every direction.

No such cry was raised during Napoleon's rule.

But what of liberty? Napoleon paid it no attention. To have given others a share in forming policy would have reduced his own authority. To have permitted freedom of the press would have invited criticism, and this he would have found intolerable. His Constitution of 1799 was the first, since the beginning of the Revolution, to omit the *Declaration of the Rights of Man and of the Citizen*. Yet, in refusing to grant political liberty he did not in any way feel that he was out of tune with the Revolution. Speaking in 1797, of the French people, he said,

. . . as for liberty, they do not understand what it means.[2]

And in conversation with Bertrand in 1821:

What France wants above all is equality.[2]

This he had provided, and so he felt justified in claiming that he and the Revolution were one.

Napoleon's viewpoint on liberty has been supported by friends and enemies alike. Albert Vandal considered that the men of 1789 did not really want political liberty. They wanted equality *and strong government*. Madame de Stäel, a confirmed opponent of Bonaparte, wrote, "Equality was the driving force of the Revolution".

If all this is true then there is something strange about the words used by Napoleon when he took power in 1799:

We want a Republic based on liberty, on equality, on the sacred principle of national representation.[2]

Swear with us the oath we have taken, to be faithful to the Republic . . . founded on equality, liberty and the representative system.

Why did the word "liberty" feature so prominently in his statements? The only possible answer is that Frenchmen were not only familiar with it but would positively welcome its inclusion. Napoleon did not use words lightly. He chose them very carefully. When we look at the history of the Revolutionary period it is clear that liberty *did* count. Men did not merely want equality, however precious that was in itself. Equality would be a means of playing a real part in political life, of making their voices heard.

Article I of the *Declaration of Rights* begins:

Men are born and remain free . . .

Article II:

The aim of every political association is the preservation of the natural and inalienable rights of man; those are liberty, property, security, and resistance to oppression.

By *resistance to oppression* was meant the sacred right of insurrection if the government became despotic. It is not surprising that Napoleon did not include the *Declaration* in his Constitution.

Article XI:

Free communication of ideas and opinions is one of the most precious rights of men. Consequently, every citizen may speak, write and print freely. . . .

In June 1792, a large crowd marched on the Assembly in Paris. One of their number addressed the representatives of the people:

Is the happiness of a free people to depend on the caprice of a king? . . . The People says NO. The People's life is worth more than that of any crowned tyrant. Liberty cannot be even temporarily deposed; but the executive power, if it fails to act, must be. It is not right that any one man should over-rule the will of twenty-five millions.

Faced by external enemies who had declared that they would destroy the Revolution, and by internal enemies who did not want a Republic, it was perhaps natural that Frenchmen should surrender some liberty in order to survive, but

as long as there had been a civilian government . . . and a Republic, there were at least the roots from which liberty might still spring, to blossom once more; now [with Napoleon] there came . . . a régime on principle opposed to liberty.[1]

---

[1] *Napoleon: For and Against* by P. Geyl (CAPE); [2] *Napoleon: Great Lives Observed* edited by M. Hutt (PRENTICE-HALL); [3] *Napoleon* by F. Markham (WEIDENFELD & NICOLSON); [4] *France on the Eve of the French Revolution* edited by J. Kaplow (WILEY); [5] *A History of Modern France* Volume 2 by A. Cobban (PENGUIN).

5

Everything for the French People

" $\mathcal{I}$ swear that I do nothing except for France," wrote Napoleon. "I have nothing in view but her advantage." There is no point in denying that Napoleon's rule was in some ways beneficial to France. But this does not mean that his fine phrases should be accepted simply because he spoke them. As always, the Legend must be approached with a critical mind.

When Bonaparte took power in 1799, government was ineffective and confused; national finances were poorly administered; civil war raged in the western Départements; religious and political differences threatened to destroy the gains of the Revolution. Within the space of a few years Napoleon had dealt successfully with each of these problems in turn. In finance his achievement was dramatic.

The Revolution . . . reformed the system of taxation on the basis of a fair contribution from all classes . . . both the assessors and collectors of the taxes had been elected by popular vote, and this arrangement has resulted in every kind of vexation, abuse and delay. Individuals were assessed more or less to their political principles. . . . In February 1793, 176 million francs were due on the year 1791 and 296 million francs on the year 1792; in the autumn of 1800 there were still 4 millions owing. But Napoleon was now in authority . . . and he made his energy felt. He himself appointed the collectors and receivers, instituted a court for the verification of their accounts . . . henceforth there are no arrears. . . . Five or six thousand officials are employed, where under the Monarchy were 200,000; and double the amount comes in.[1]

Napoleon could rightly claim that he had "dragged the State out of the morass of bankruptcy".

The Bank of France, set up in 1800, helped to stabilize the value of the currency by limiting the issue of banknotes which were not backed up by gold. Good management and honesty were introduced to local government. On 25 December 1799, Napoleon addressed a note to his brother Lucien, Minister for Home Affairs.

*Since 1790, the 36,000 local bodies have been like 36,000 orphan girls
. . . they have been neglected or defrauded for the past 10 years. . . . A
new set of Mayors . . . or Municipal Councillors has generally meant
nothing more than a fresh form of robbery; they have stolen the by-road,'
stolen the footpath, stolen the timber, robbed the church, and filched the
property of the Commune; and this looting is still going on. . . . The
Minister will therefore begin by having a general inventory made of the
36,000 Communes . . . once this inventory is drawn up, the Prefects and
sub-Prefects will be warned . . . to get rid of any Mayors . . . who do not
see eye to eye with them as to local improvement and regeneration.*[2]

On a purely administrative level, most historians would agree with
Cobban that "of the general ability of the Prefects and the valuable
work they did in restoring administrative good habits . . . there can be
no question".

The Civil Constitution of the Clergy, introduced in July
1790, had laid down that Bishops and lower clergy were to be elected
by the people, and paid by the State—to which they were required to
swear allegiance. This had divided the French church, since many
priests refused to accept the Civil Constitution. It was a division which
reached into almost every parish in the country. Opposition priests
often became associated with political groups which aimed at the
overthrow of the Revolution. On this account the western Départements of France were ravaged by civil war. By the Concordat of 1801,
negotiated with the Pope, Napoleon restored stability to religious
relationships within France.

Ineffective government during the Directory (1795–99) had
led to widespread brigandage in the rural areas. Napoleon set up a
gendarmerie of 52 Brigades to deal with the problem. Men of all
shades of political and religious opinion were given position and office
under the new régime. In this way a greater sense of unity was created.
It did not need a legend to convince Frenchmen that Napoleon was
stating fact when he said,

I have closed the gaping abyss of anarchy and have unscrambled chaos.

Throughout his reign, from all corners of Europe, Bonaparte
sent instructions to his ministers on the good government and development of the nation. On 1 March 1805 he was urging that agriculture
be stimulated; on 28 March he was demanding that information be
produced on the state of schools, roads and harvests. On 2 September
1807 he was insisting that standards be maintained in industry; on
21 December 1808 he was laying plans for waterworks in Paris. A
note of 5 September 1810 on prison reform began:

What we want to aim at, in general, is that the prisoners should be healthy, and the prisons clean, and that those who have been sentenced should be kept apart from those who have only been charged.[2]

An instruction of 2 May 1811 concerned work for the unemployed, and one of 11 March 1812 laid plans for the provision of soup-kitchens and other relief for the poor. Major work in the field of codification produced the Civil Code of 1805, the Code of Civil Procedure in 1806, the Commercial Code in 1807, the Code of Criminal Instruction in 1808 and the Penal Code in 1810. Bonaparte has been rightly praised for effecting an achievement which has stood the test of time.

In Napoleon's view, French life and society had, by 1799, been reduced to "sand"—unsettled, loose, blown about in any wind which might rise. He therefore felt it his duty "to throw upon the soil of France a few blocks of granite". A nagging doubt remains that much in French life and society was undeservedly suffocated or crushed beneath these blocks of granite. Whilst the ordered life of a community cannot exist without a degree of stability, too much stability can have a stifling effect. Even his admirers could feel that Napoleon sometimes went too far. In Stendhal's view, the Prefects were established

. . . to humble the citizen and above all to prevent him from discussing matters.[3]

Before the Empire was four years old, France had a University, a number of technical institutions and well over 1000 secondary schools. At first sight this appears a worthy achievement, without doubt in the interests of France. But why was it done, and with what results? An Imperial Decree stated:

All the schools of the University will take as the basis of their instruction fidelity to the Emperor, to the Imperial Monarchy, the Guardian of the Happiness of the nations, and to the Napoleonic Dynasty, the Preserver of the Unity of France.

The educational system was designed to produce propaganda favourable to the Emperor. One of his better known remarks on education was "Young people can hardly avoid accepting whatever version of the facts is presented to them". Every detail was carefully considered. "These are the masters they need," declared Napoleon, as he selected the books to be read in schools, "for they navigate with the sails of obedience".

The free expression of opinion was not tolerated in Napoleonic France. "I shall never allow the press to say anything contrary to my interests." When he became First Consul there were about 73 political newspapers in Paris. By a Decree of 17 January 1800 he suppressed 60.

By the end of 1800 only 9 political papers appeared in the capital, and by 1811 only 4 were allowed to circulate. An Imperial Circular of 1807 limited the provincial press to one newspaper per Département— and it was to be edited by the Prefect. In 1810, 97 of the 157 printing presses in Paris were closed down. Anything which challenged Napoleon's view of himself was in danger. On 7 May 1806 the Minister of Police received an instruction:

> *Millot has just published a 4th volume, containing all kinds of ridiculous nonsense, and depreciating our victories. It is the height of indecency that such an ignoramus should write in the grand manner about contemporary events. Have the book suppressed . . .*[2]

Many would agree that through such activities Napoleon ". . . had given France . . . a steel corset", and that "political life was frozen into silence".

And what of his military adventures? Were they in the interests of France? Of course they brought glory. They also brought disaster. And where does the balance lie? Between 1800 and 1812, 1,400,000 Frenchmen were conscripted. In 1813, after the losses in Russia, 800,000 were called-up, and in 1814 another 100,000. Of just over 2 million men drawn into Napoleon's armies, about 500,000 were either killed or wounded. It is frequently argued that such losses were slight when compared with the 1,360,000 French soldiers killed in the four years of the 1914–18 war. It is certainly useful to keep in mind that war in the nineteenth century produced fewer casualties than war in the twentieth century. But this does not answer the question: Was the killing or wounding of half a million men good for France?

In the last years of the Empire, France had had her fill of war. When he crossed the border from Spain in November 1813, Wellington reported:

> *All except the officials are sick of Bonaparte, because there is no prospect of peace with him.*

In December 1813, the Legislative Assembly, showing a remarkable and unusual independence, voted 235/51 to make the following statement:

> *Our ills are at their height. The Patrie is threatened at all points of the frontier; we are suffering from a destitution unexampled in the whole history of the state. Commerce is destroyed, industry dying. . . . What are the causes of these unutterable miseries? A vexatious administration . . . and even crueller excesses practised for the recruitment of the armies. . . . A barbarous and endless war swallows up periodically the youth torn from education, agriculture, commerce, and the arts.*

Even after Waterloo, Napoleon was prepared to continue the war, whatever the cost. Does this support his claim?

Whatever We have done, We have done for the . . . welfare of Our people.[2]

And in the end, because of his unwillingness to fade from the picture, the allies exacted a severer peace settlement from France. . . .

Even with regard to those areas where Napoleon's work was clearly beneficial to France, it is possible to argue that he was motivated by self-interest rather than national interest. May it not have been that behind his desire for stability was the wish to have a sound base for his military adventures? If France benefited in some respects it could have been that this benefit was incidental to Napoleon's real aim—to consolidate his power at home in order to make the task of military conquest in Europe so much easier.

---

[1]*Revolution and Reaction in Modern France* by G. L. Dickinson (ALLEN & UNWIN); [2]*Napoleon Bonaparte* letters translated by J. M. Thompson (DENT); [3]*A Life of Napoleon* by H. B. Stendhal (THE RONDALE PRESS)

6

The Liberator

he nineteenth century was a period of great nationalist movements. Large, independent, unified nations were created in areas where previously there had been a clutter of small and separate states. The two most obvious examples are the Italian Kingdom, created between 1859 and 1871, and the German Empire, built up between 1866 and 1871. The Legend claims that Napoleon consciously set out, in his foreign policy, to free peoples from old tyrannies in order that they might move forward to freedom within their own independent nation states. Under French rule, they would develop a sense of dignity and importance and come to realize that their future lay in joining with people of the same language in one unified state. In Vandal's words,

Napoleon tried to propel the nations faster along the road of their destiny.[1]

There is no doubt that there *is* a connection between the Age of Napoleon and the Age of Nationalism, particularly with regard to Italy and Germany. Through conquest and annexation "he enormously simplified the map in both of them".

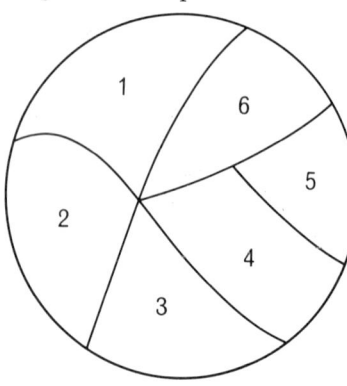

Suppose, for example, that before being annexed by Napoleon's France, a territory was made up of six small, independent states. Although the people in all six areas might speak the same language, there would be different administrations in each state, and different laws. Furthermore, each was kept apart from the others by customs barriers so that freedom of trade was impossible.

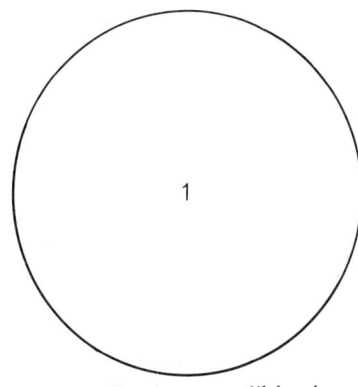

Conquest and annexation produced almost immediately a single state with one government, one administration, one set of laws, and no internal tariff barriers to interfere with trading and communication.

Developments of this kind were bound to start some men thinking of a future, not too far off, in which this could be the normal pattern.

Furthermore "his victories enabled French ideas to sweep the continent".

Wherever he ruled or placed his rulers, the inquisition, feudal rights, all exclusive privileges were abolished . . . customs barriers between provinces thrown down . . . all sorts of inequalities, he took his sword and cut. . . .[1]

The principle of the career open to the talents was exported to the conquered areas. In a letter to brother Jerome, ruler of Westphalia, Napoleon wrote:

What is above all desired in Germany is that you will grant to those who do not belong to the nobility, but possess talents, an equal claim to offices, and that all vestiges of serfdom and of barriers between the sovereign and the lowest class of the people should be completely done away with. . . . Legal procedure in open court, the jury, these are the points by which your Monarchy should be distinguished. . . . Your people must enjoy a liberty, an equality, a prosperity.[2]

There is, however, another side. The conquered areas were at times treated with a marked lack of respect, and often with considerable brutality. It is difficult to reconcile the Legend of a Liberator with the fact that wherever French armies marched, censorship followed. In Baden, for instance, only one newspaper was allowed, and it was edited by Napoleon's officials. In 1811 a decree laid down that any newspaper in the Confederation of the Rhine which printed political news not in *Le Moniteur* would be suppressed. In Italy, newspapers were not allowed to criticize the French. If peoples under French control did not follow the strict letter of Napoleon's commands they could expect harsh treatment.

I think it ridiculous, wrote Bonaparte to Jerome, *that you should make an argument of the opposition of the Westphalian people. If the people decline their own happiness they only show their anarchical inclinations. They are guilty, and the ruler's first duty is to punish them.*[3]

In a letter to Murat, in 1806, just after he had created his brother-in-law Grand Duke of Berg, Napoleon wrote:

I am astonished that the notables of Cleves have refused to swear allegiance to you. Let them take the oath within 24 hours or have them arrested, bring them to trial, and confiscate their possessions.[1]

Clearly it was not Napoleon's intention that the peoples of Europe should show any sign of independence. When his Italian subjects complained about the level of taxation he wrote, angrily, in April 1806:

. . . my Italian subjects know me too well to forget that there is more in my little finger than in all their heads put together. In Paris, where people are more enlightened than in Italy, they hold their tongues, and bow to the judgment of a man who has proved that he saw further and more clearly than they did.[2]

A similar communication was addressed to the Lieutenant General of the Emperor in Holland on 25 September 1810:

You speak to me of the grievances of the Amsterdam folk, of their anxieties, and of their discontent. . . . I shall do what suits the interests of my Empire. I despise the clamour of madmen who think they know my interests better than I know them myself. . . . I did not take over the government of Holland in order to consult the common people of Amsterdam or to do what other people want. . . .[2]

Where men wrote or spoke openly against French domination the penalties were severe. In the German Confederation the bookseller, Palm, was executed, as was Andreas Hofer in Naples. When a minor revolt took place in Hesse in 1807, Napoleon instructed his military commander in the area:

My intention is that the main village where the insurrection started shall be burnt and that thirty of the ringleaders shall be shot; an impressive example is needed to contain the hatred of the peasantry. . . . If you have not yet made an example, let there be one without delay. . . . Let not the month pass without the principal village or small town which gave the signal for insurrection being burned, and a large number of individuals shot. . . .

Francisco Goya depicted his impressions of the relationships between the local inhabitants and the French invader during the Peninsular War. This was part of the reality which lay behind Napoleon's address to the people of Spain:

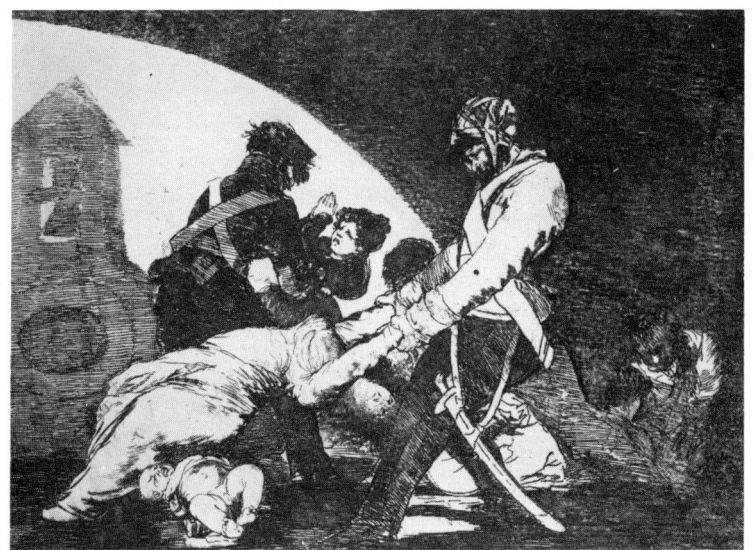

In this aquatint Goya graphically depicts the French soldiers' treatment of Spanish civilians.

Your grandchildren will bless me as a regenerator. The day when I appeared in your midst, they will count among the most memorable.

The pride of conquered people was constantly offended by what seemed French arrogance in claiming that they had come "to civilize"; offended by the way in which local habits and customs were discarded; offended by economic exploitation. Of French administration in Dalmatia, on the east coast of the Adriatic, Pisari wrote:

A people's legislation is the product of its habits, its traditions, its history, even of the nature of its soil. France was, in those days, too proud of its laws to be able to admit that they might not answer the needs of all times and all peoples. . . . The result was that this population was turned to rebellion.[1]

It would have been remarkable had Napoleon allowed the foreigners under his control to say or do as they pleased; to rebel at will; to conduct guerrilla warfare without suffering reprisals. This is not the way in which conquerors can be expected to behave. Yet this is not the point in question. The Legend claims that Napoleon was the Liberator of Europe. In many respects the reality was quite different.

[1] *Napoleon: For and Against* by P. Geyl (CAPE); [2] *Napoleon Bonaparte* letters translated by J. M. Thompson (DENT); [3] *NCMH* Volume IX

Further Sources

Documentary Sources

Napoleon: Great Lives Observed ed. M. Hutt (PRENTICE-HALL)
Napoleon Bonaparte letters translated from French by J. M. Thompson (DENT)

Reference

Napoleon: For and Against Pieter Geyl (CAPE)
New Cambridge Modern History Volume IX

General Reading

The First European Revolution Norman Hampson (THAMES & HUDSON)
The Age of Napoleon Christopher Herold (PENGUIN)
Napoleon Felix Markham (WEIDENFELD & NICOLSON)
Revolutionary Europe 1783-1815 George Rudé (FONTANA)
Napoleon and Europe L. C. F. Turner (WARNE)

Campaigns (for sketch maps)

Europe 1789–1914: A Sketchmap Textbook Dudley Woodget (LONGMAN)
The Peninsular War R. J. Wilkinson Latham (SHIRE PUBLICATIONS)
Borodino and the War of 1812 Christopher Duffy (SPHERE)

Fiction

The *Hornblower* novels by C. S. Forrester have as a background the Revolutionary and Napoleonic Wars.

R. F. Delderfield's *Seven Men of Gascony* is set in the context of the campaigns between 1809 and 1815. As Delderfield comments:

> Most of the incidents recorded in the following pages are true, episodes written down at the time, or in after years, by the officers and men of the Grand Army.

Dennis Wheatley's *Roger Brooke* novels are also of interest.

Assignments

Chapter 1—The Legend

1. The Commission of 1854, set up "to collect, classify and publish the correspondence" of Napoleon, had failed to please his nephew. He was, however, satisfied with the declaration made by the new editors when they began their work in 1864.

In general we have taken as our guide the simple idea that we were called to publish what the Emperor would have published, if, surveying himself, and anticipating the verdict of history, he had wanted to display his person and system to posterity.

What problems would the material published by such editors present for the historian wanting to know the "truth" about Napoleon?

2. Explain why one of the following letters would be included and the other omitted by the 1864 editors.

a. Napoleon in conversation with Melzi D'Eril, Milan, 1797
The Republic is a fancy of which the French are at present full, but it will pass away like all the others. What they want is glory and gratified vanity; but as for liberty, they do not understand what it means. . . . Give them baubles—that suffices them; they will be amused and will let themselves be led, so long as the end towards which they are going is skilfully hidden from them.

b. Napoleon's Proclamation to The Inhabitants of Western France, December 1799
Unjust laws have been passed and executed; arbitrary acts have undermined the security of the citizen and the liberty of conscience. . . . To repair these errors and injustices a government founded on the sacred principles of liberty, equality and the representative system has been proclaimed. . . . It will be the constant desire of (this government) to heal all the wounds of France.

1. From his headquarters in northern Italy, Napoleon sent the following dispatch to the Directory in August 1796. It gives brief accounts of the strengths and weaknesses of fourteen of his generals. Read each comment carefully and then, using as many of Napoleon's opinions as possible, piece together the various qualities he would wish to see in the "perfect general".

I think it worthwhile to give you my opinion of the generals serving with this army. . . .

BERTHIER: ability, energy, courage, character; everything in his favour

AUGEREAU: plenty of character, courage, firmness, energy; is accustomed to war, popular with his men, lucky in the field

MASSÉNA: active, tireless, enterprising, grasps a situation and makes up his mind quickly

SERURIER: . . . dislikes responsibility . . . has too poor an opinion of his men. . . .

DESPINOY: dull, slack, unenterprising; doesn't understand war, is unpopular with the men, doesn't use his head. . . .

SAURET: . . . not enough education for a general; unlucky

ABBATUCCI: not fit to command fifty men

GARNIER, MEUNIER, CASABIANCA: incapable; unfit to command a battalion on such an active and serious campaign

MACQUART: no ability; lively

GAULTIER: all right for a clerical job; has never seen a shot fired

VAUBOIS, SAHUGUET: . . . were on garrison duty, and have only just become listed for active service. . . . They have done very well in the duties so far assigned them; but the example of General Despinoy, who did very well at Milan, and very badly at the head of his division, compels me to judge men by their actual performance.

2. After his victory at Lodi (10 May 1796) Napoleon heard from the Government that Kellerman, the victor of Valmy, was to share his command. On 14 May Napoleon wrote the following letter:

I am writing to the Directory about this idea of dividing the command . . . Kellerman would command the army quite as well as I do . . . but I am convinced that to combine Kellerman and myself in Italy would be to court disaster. I cannot willingly serve alongside a man who considers himself the best general in Europe. In any case, I am certain that one bad general is better than two good ones.

a. What connection do you see between the passages which are underlined?

b. What point do you think Napoleon is making in the final sentence?

3. Imagine that you are a member of a French Balloon Unit observing the battlefield of Waterloo.

What suggestions would you make to the Emperor about the troops under the command of

a. General d'Erlon

b. Marshal Grouchy?

Chapter 3—All in Self-defence

(Simulation for groups of eight, made up of rulers of Austria, Britain, Prussia and Russia, each with an adviser.)

1. Napoleon has escaped from Elba, has returned to Paris, and has issued the following circular letter.

TO THE SOVEREIGNS OF EUROPE

Paris, 4 April 1815

Monsieur, My Brother,

You will have learnt, during the course of the last month, of my landing again in France, of my entry into Paris, and of the departure of the Bourbon family. . . . The re-establishment of the Imperial Throne was necessary for the happiness of Frenchmen; my dearest hope is that it may also secure repose for the whole of Europe . . . I have provided the world in the past with a programme of great contests; it will please me better in future to acknowledge no rivalry but that of the advocates of peace, and no combat but a crusade for the felicity of mankind. It is France's pleasure to make a frank avowal of this noble ideal. Jealous of her independence, she will always base her policy upon an unqualified respect for the independence of other peoples.

If your Majesty's personal sentiments—as I confidently trust—are the same, there is assurance of a widespread and long continued repose; and justice, seated on the confines of the various states, will be competent to guard their frontiers. I eagerly embrace this opportunity to repeat the sentiments of sincere esteem and perfect friendship with which I remain,

Monsieur My Brother,

Your Good Brother,

Napoleon.

Each group should prepare a Bulletin, addressed to Napoleon, detailing the reasons why the circular letter has been accepted or rejected.

Chapter 5—Everything for the French People

1. On 13 January 1809 Napoleon addressed the following note to Count Fouché, Minister of Police.

Now that we are in 1809, I think it would be useful to have some articles written, in good style, contrasting the misfortunes from which France has suffered in the past with the prosperous state of the Empire in 1809. The comparison should be worked out under several heads . . . territory . . . internal welfare, international prestige, finance, etc. You have got men competent to write five or six good articles on this very important subject, and to give public opinion a lead in the right direction.

a. Why do you think Napoleon used the phrases which have been underlined?

b. Imagine that you are one of the "competent" persons mentioned in the note. Write a short article which would have been acceptable to Napoleon.